Dorothy McRae-McMahon is a minister in the Uniting Church in Australia. For ten years she was a minister with the Pitt Street Uniting Church in the centre of Sydney and then for five years the National Director for Mission for her church. She was a member of the World Council of Churches Worship Committee for its Canberra Assembly and Moderator of its Worship Committee for the Harare Assembly. She is now active in the Uniting Church in South Sydney, co-edits the *South Sydney Herald* and writes liturgy.

Her community awards indicate her interests and concerns. She has received a Jubilee Medal from the Queen for work with women in NSW (1977), an Australian Government Peace Award (1986), the Australian Human Rights Medal (1988) and an Honorary Doctorate of Letters from Macquarie University in Sydney for work with minorities and her contribution to the spiritual life of the community (1992).

Also by the author

Being Clergy, Staying Human
(Alban Institute, Washington, Australia, 1992)

Echoes of Our Journey: Liturgies of the People
(Joint Board of Christian Education, Melbourne, 1993)

The Glory of Blood, Sweat and Tears: Liturgies for Living and Dying
(Joint Board of Christian Education, Melbourne, 1996)

Everyday Passions: A Conversation on Living
(ABC Books, Sydney, 1998)

Liturgies for the Journey of Life
(SPCK, 2000)

Prayers for Life's Particular Moments
(SPCK and Desbooks, 2001)

Daring Leadership in the 21st Century
(ABC Books, Sydney, 2001)

In This Hour: Liturgies for Pausing
(SPCK and Desbooks, 2002)

Rituals for Life, Love and Loss
(Jane Curry Publishing, 2003)

Memoirs of Moving On
(Jane Curry Publishing, 2004)

Liturgies for Daily Life
(SPCK, 2004)

Worship for the Young in Years
(MediaCom, 2005)

LITURGIES FOR HIGH DAYS

Dorothy McRae-McMahon

First published in Great Britain in 2006

Society for Promoting Christian Knowledge
36 Causton Street
London SW1P 4ST

British Library Cataloguing-in-Publication Data
A catalogue record for this book is available from the British Library

ISBN-13: 978–0–281–05874–7
ISBN-10: 0–281–05874–1

1 3 5 7 9 10 8 6 4 2

Typeset by Kenneth Burnley, Wirral, Cheshire
Printed in Great Britain by Ashford Colour Press

Contents

Contents

Introduction

Even though we celebrate, or prepare for, basically the same events in each church year on the 'high days', I have found over the years that they can be brought alive by focusing on a specific theme within the central message. It is often helpful to sit with parishioners, read out the Bible passages for the period or day and invite them to see if there is a particular theme emerging for them. After each person has shared his or her theme, the group can discuss which one stands out for them. In this process, I have noticed that the theme for that year is often subconsciously or consciously related to the way the congregation is feeling about its life or the life around it at that point. People tend to pick up a particular word from the passage which is most significant for them for some current reason. If you then proceed to use their theme, the season comes alive for them in a new way.

We have often used this way of preparing liturgy in our congregation of South Sydney Uniting Church, which is set in one of the most struggling areas of Australia. Sometimes members of the congregation also work on imagery for symbolic acts during periods like Advent and Lent and this enhances their ownership of, and participation in, the services. You will see some of their work in this book.

The seasons of the church year may come around year after year but they never fail to carry me through pathways that challenge, renew and lead me on into a different future. As I celebrate each period, I also experience a sense of being gathered into the community of the universal church in all its situations and places. As I write, I embrace again the people with whom I have worshipped over the years in Australia and New Zealand, Kenya, Zimbabwe, Cyprus, Lebanon, Britain, Switzerland, India, Hong Kong, Japan, the Philippines, Singapore, Malaysia, Indonesia, Sri Lanka and the United States.

Thanks be to God for all that unites us on these our holy days.

Dorothy McRae-McMahon

Using these liturgies

Most of these services are prepared in relation to the lectionary readings from the Revised Common Lectionary. Having said that, some of the services that are attached to certain readings may well be used in other contexts and with other readings. Some of the liturgies for periods like Advent and Lent are in the form of one basic liturgy running through that period, sometimes with differing responses to the word each week, while others are separate liturgies for each Sunday of the season.

All of these liturgies would benefit by the inclusion of music. I have left it for the users to decide what music they will add and at what point. Music is a very cultural thing, even in the church these days. There are now very few 'well-known hymns' and sung responses!

When I am making suggestions about symbols or symbolic acts in a service, I have noted the main resources needed. However, I always assume that people will add their own ideas in preparing the environment for liturgical events – that they will bring in their own contextual images or symbols, or anything else that might enhance the moment. I tend to keep symbolic acts simple, as I have found that inhibits worship from becoming a 'performance'. I also mainly keep to a relatively small number of symbols like candles, water, earth, oil, stones, flowers and cloths, as I have discovered that they do not really lose effectiveness in being used repeatedly and it avoids gimmickry.

The way the suggested symbolic acts are used will, of course, depend on the size of the congregation concerned. If it is large, it may be necessary to arrange for some people to act on behalf of the congregation rather than issuing a general invitation. I also assume that some people may prefer to take out the symbolic acts altogether and simply adapt the prayers. If the congregation does not normally use printed responsive liturgies, people can be allocated to give leadership, sometimes using more than one voice.

Obviously all good leaders of worship decide what suits their church culture and practice. We all take the ideas of others and evolve and adapt for best use. I do the same myself!

Acknowledgements

I would like to thank the people of the South Sydney Uniting Church for all their gifts of life and grace to me, and SPCK for enabling me to share my liturgies with others.

CHRIST THE KING

Melody of harmony in all the universe,
sound of singing as the people learn to love
and soaring of hope in every needy child,
wind of change for justice,
rhythm in the beating of the hearts which care
and breath in the silent hope of the frail survivals:
God of all kindness,
Christ who reigns in justice.
We gather here before you.

Hail to Christ, the King

Call to worship

Hail to Christ, the King,
ruler who lays down the power to destroy,
leader who treads through the costly journey
and into the shadow places of life,
that we might find the rising of life before us:
Hail to Christ, the King,
born to be first witness to God's truth,
whose might lies in mercy,
whose throne is placed in the midst of humble people.
Hail to Christ, the King.

Prayer of invocation

Even as we bow before your holy presence, O Christ,
we pray that you will be found among us in this place.
Open our eyes that we may see glimpses of your glory,
glory which spans the ages,
wonder of risen life which touches us with the gentle hand
    of grace.
Be known to us, Holy Jesus, through the power of your Spirit.
Amen.

Prayer of confession

Jesus Christ, even as we commit ourselves to follow you,
we own that we do not always give you that authority in our lives.
We choose to elevate ourselves to higher status
and exercise our own power in the church and the world.
In humility and hope, we name who we are before you:

Silent reflection

We are human, not divine, O God.
Restore us to right relationship with you, Jesus Christ.

We confess, O God,
that sometimes we imagine that, as Christians,
we are superior to others,
glorying in the knowledge that you have given us salvation,
as though that makes us more than human.

Silent reflection

We are human, not divine, O God.
Restore us to right relationship with you, Jesus Christ.

Then there are times when we doubt
that your reign is established in the world,
when it is hard for us to see how that could be
and how to participate in that reign.

Silent reflection

We are human, not divine, O God.
Restore us to right relationship with you, Jesus Christ.
For we pray in your name.
Amen.

Words of assurance

Christ is the King. We are never condemned.
The universe resounds with the gracious voice of our God.
We are forgiven! This is the word of our God and sovereign.
Thanks be to God.

Prayer of thanksgiving

We give thanks, O God,
that Jesus remodels for us the role of those who lead.
In Jesus we see a royal one who walks in vulnerability,
suffering with the people,
loving us in immeasurable grace,

bringing all to the wonder of the fullness of life,
in freedom and hope.
Thank you, O God, for the wonder of this gift to us.
Amen.

Readings

2 Samuel 23.1–7; Psalm 132.1–12; Revelation 1.4b–8; John 18.33–37

Sermon

Offering

Prayer of intercession

In awe, we contemplate your majesty, O Christ.
As we bring our prayers to you this day,
we first hold silence
that we may know more fully who we are and who you are
and listen for the insights of your Holy Spirit:

A silence is kept

As you touch our hearts with care,
calling us towards a more generous love for the world,
a braver dream for the future
and a creative possibility for our part in that,
we bring our particular prayers to you:

The people pray

O God, we hear the call, 'O come, all you faithful'
as it rings down the years and sounds in the songs of hope
for a world in which the little and the least
join the melody of joy.
**May we be the music of your life in the world,
resounding with a great new hope
for better things to come,
for steadfast faith in the possibility of your reign of love,
for the offering of glimpses of a different future**

when the whole creation owns your truth.
Amen.

Commissioning

Go forth as the loyal servants of the servant King,
and show the world the glory of the one who saves us for others.

Benediction

And may that which is of God be enthroned in our hearts,
that which is of the Spirit reach out towards those who long
 for love
and that which is of the Creator be found among our company.
Amen.

A different reign

Call to worship

Christ whose reign is born in suffering,
tested in travail
and speaking through the integrity of woundedness:
We come in awe and thanksgiving.

Jesus, Child of our humanity,
authentic whether in wilderness or weddings,
treading our earth in vulnerable truth:
We come in awe and thanksgiving.

God who reigns in gentleness,
Christ who never gives us up,
Jesus who embraces all who come in faith:
We come in awe and thanksgiving this day.

Prayer of invocation

Touch us in our fragile hope, Holy One.
Reach us in our hiddenness and guilt.
Seek us when we are afraid to be found.
Come, Jesus the Christ, come and give to us your life.
Amen.

Prayer of confession

It is hard to bring our confession to you, Jesus Christ.
There are no words which can do justice
to this moment as we stand before your costly journey.
We know that you carry in your life
all the pain and wrongs which lie in our life
and yet you reach out to us.
In the silence, we wait for you to know us:

A silence is kept

You know who we are this day, O God.
Grieve with us, Jesus Christ, as we face ourselves.
Weep with us as we remember who you call us to be.
Stay with us in the loneliness of emptiness and doubt
which you find within us now.

A silence is kept

We are no different from those who required your death long ago.
We too betray you.
We too leave you alone when we are afraid.
Forgive us, O God,
and restore us to your love.
Amen.

Words of assurance

Even as he suffers in the depths of the pain
of all that we deliver to life,
the Christ forgives us, reassuring all who come in hope.
We are forgiven!
Thanks be to God.

Prayer of thanksgiving

We thank you, O God,
that you give to us a different royalty,
one which is bereft of privilege and wealth,
one whose power lies in truth,
in faithfulness and in grace for all people.
We thank you, Jesus Christ,
that you did not waver from your calling,
as you entered into the pain of our life
yet leapt free of all its bondages.
Thank you, O God, for all that you are in Jesus.
Amen.

Readings

Jeremiah 23.1–6; Luke 1.68–79; Colossians 1.11–20; Luke 23.33–43

Sermon

Prayer of intercession

O God, there are so many situations in our world
which seem to defy the power of the reign of Christ.
We see before us violence and injustice
and tyranny and oppression in the lives of so many people.
We pray for the empowering of all who work for good
in these countries and among these people:

The people pray

Hear our prayers, O God.
Show to us new ways of sharing in these struggles.
Give to us ideas which make clearer our part
in changing the world around us.
Fill us with courage and faith as we try to stand with you
in every place and for all people.

And now we pray for ourselves,
for all here who wait in longing for better things to come.
We pray for those who grieve the loss of those they love,
or who hope for life which is stronger and freer.
We pray for our church
that we may be known as your true witnesses,
and as those who love our neighbours as ourselves.
This we pray in your name, Christ the King.
Amen.

Commissioning

Go into the world as those who follow
the King of justice and peace.
Go in hope and faith,
believing that the reign of God will surely come.

Benediction

God will bless us,
Christ will hold us
and the Holy Spirit will bring us grace.
Amen.

ADVENT

Sing songs of hope into the waiting air
and begin the dance of joy,
for the life of faith is before us.
Look into the distance and see the rising dawn
with shining rays in acts of love
and warming brightness from the heart of God.

Joyful anticipation

For this service you will need

- *A purple cloth flowing from the communion table like a pathway towards the congregation*
- *A basket of buds on the table*

Call to worship

Mary's song is joined with the voice of Isaiah
and with our own melodies of hope.
The deserts of the harsh summers will blossom again,
the cool waters will flow into parched lives.
The dread cold of winter will be warmed by creative love
and those who have been pushed to the edges of the world
will sit in the centre of the feast.
Our waiting is coming to an end,
the time is near for the great thanksgiving,
the welcome to the God who is with us for ever.
Let us worship God!

Prayer of invocation

From the prisons of our life struggles, we ask our anxious
    question, O God:
Are we still waiting for our salvation, or will it be present here today?
Show us the joys of healing and faith and justice
which are the signs of your life among us,
that we may bear our witness to the world in hope.
Be with us this day in truth, O Jesus Christ.
Amen.

Prayer of confession

Dear God, you for whom we always wait,
have patience with our anxious hearts.
When we are anxious because
we are not sure that we know the way
and become paralysed in our doubts:
Turn us towards your eternal faithfulness, O God.

If we rush hither and thither looking for another sign,
another inspiration, another leader, another idea,
instead of staying quietly before you
and facing what it means to take up our cross and follow you:
Turn us towards your eternal faithfulness, O God.

When we create communities of faith which are anything
but witnesses to our joyful expectation,
which crush delight, rarely laugh
and fail to live with the fullness which you offer to us:
Turn us towards your eternal faithfulness, O God.
Forgive us and bring us to your true life again.
Amen.

Words of assurance

The warm life of Jesus Christ never runs cold,
never becomes hardened in judgement.
Even as Christ grieves with us, love is moving towards us.
We are forgiven. We are offered the joy of salvation!
Thanks be to God!
Amen.

Prayer of thanksgiving

In joyful anticipation we walk towards the truth of your coming,
    O Christ.
With sighs of thanksgiving we raise our heads above the trials of life
and see the sunrise of your arrival on the horizons of our world.
Our hearts are filled with gratitude for this, the gift of the Messiah.
Thanks be to you, O God.
Amen.

Readings

Isaiah 35.1–10; Psalm 146.5–10; Luke 1.46–55; James 5.7–10

Sermon

Prayers of intercession

The world is always waiting for you, O God,
always calling for its saviour,
always hoping that the next person it meets
will be the one who will transform life and lift the burdens from
    its shoulders.
We bring our prayers for those
who are crying out in longing on this day, loving God.
We pray for our lost children,
for those who are addicted, abused and homeless,
and who are then destroyed again as they wander the streets
in loneliness and vulnerability.
Help us to be your sign of hope for them, O God.

We pray for places where there seem to be so many cycles of
    violence and hate,
where we fear that wars and wounding will never cease
as though each generation is infected
by the pains and sins of the generation before:

The places are named

It is hard to believe that anything could change
to save these people and places, O God,
but still we pray:
Help us to be your sign of hope for them, O God.

Then we pray for ourselves, that our lifting of the heart,
in response to your coming will shine forth from this place
that the blind will see and the lame will leap in new life
as we wait for the coming of your peace.
Help us to be your sign of hope here, O God.
Amen.

Response to the word

In response to the word, let us reflect on any small signs of hope which we can see for a more just and loving world or in the lives of people around us.

Silent reflection

Now I invite you, if you wish, to take a bud from the table, place it on the pathway cloth and in a word or phrase name the sign of hope you have seen and which we could celebrate for the future.

The people do so

We have seen these glimpses of your coming, O Christ.
We hold them in our hands in delight
as we commit ourselves to add to them each day.
Amen.

Commissioning

Let us leave this place in joyful expectation,
carrying with us the stories of our salvation,
that the world may know the Christ and be glad.

Benediction

And may the blessing of the coming of the Christ
flow forth into all the world
as the angel voices prepare to sing their songs
and the God who lifted the heart of Mary come among us,
on this day and the next.
Amen.

The dawning of new life –
the leap for joy

Call to worship

Deep within the universe,
there is a leap of joy,
a quivering of hope,
and a trembling dream:
For the Christ is coming.

Even as the dark greets the coming dawn,
so the hearts of the people stir in wondering expectation:
For the Christ is coming.
Let us worship our God.

Prayer of invocation

Speak into the sounding of new beginnings,
lying deep within our life together, Holy Spirit of God.
Move within us with the healing touch of your life,
reaching towards ours as we gather here.
Make your presence known in this hour we pray, Jesus Christ.
Amen.

Prayer of confession

O God, if in the face of these troubling times
we have gone drearily on,
putting one foot in front of the other,
dutifully doing what we must do each day, even on Sunday:
We are sorry for our lack of joy, passionate Jesus.
Forgive us for our failure to look with expectation
for your surprises, O God.

Silent reflection

The dawning of new life

If we have become boring people,
assuming that there is little more to debate
and no new conceptions in the womb of life
which may bring to birth an exciting adventure of faith
in our ambiguous and challenging journey with you, O God:
We are sorry for our lack of joy, passionate Jesus.
Forgive us for our failure to look with expectation
for your surprises, O God.

Silent reflection

If we crush, or look with cynicism
on the radiant new faith of others,
or fail to notice and learn from
the innocent delight of children:
We are sorry for our lack of joy, passionate Jesus.
Forgive us for our failure to look with expectation
for your surprises, O God.

Silent reflection

Forgive us and come to us in grace, Jesus Christ.
Amen.

Words of assurance

The love of Christ refuses to be defeated
by the apathy of anyone.
It leaps with joy and pours grace upon our heads,
here and now and in this place.
We are forgiven!
Thanks be to God.

Prayer of thanksgiving

Joy is coming!
Thanks be to God.

Within human life the Spirit stirs
as it prepares for the labouring,

and the preparation for the emerging of love.
Thanks be to God.

The mystery of birth,
the engagement of God with all that we are,
is waiting for its golden dawning
in the hopeful hearts of the people.
Thanks be to God.
We will wait in faith for the Christ to come.
Amen.

Readings

Micah 5.2–5a; Psalm 80.1–7; Hebrews 10.5–10; Luke 1.39–45

Sermon

Affirmation of faith

In response to the word, let us stand and affirm our faith together:
We believe that, even in the waiting,
the creation stirs with unseen hope,
with seeds of Godly life in prophetic forms
and the brave truths of the Spirit.

We believe in a God
who never fails to lift our hearts,
and to hold before us
greater dreams, grander visions
and deeper hopes than we will ever know.
This we believe
and from this we will live.

Prayer of intercession

Dear God, we pray today that, as we look around us,
both here and wider in the world,
we will be able to see the early signs of new life

in people and places,
the beginnings and growings of things
which could lead to changes, to justice, to peace
and to your love coming forth in new ways among us.

Silent reflection

We pray that we will prepare the way for what could be,
rather than settling for what now is,
that, just as Mary saw herself as blessed among women,
so we will see ourselves as blessed among people
because we are chosen to share
in the bringing of your true life before the world
and its longing peoples.

Silent reflection

Come, Child Jesus, come.
Come, carrying our innocent hopes,
come, bearing glad news to the world,
come, filled for ever with love and grace,
delight of the humble who find you,
and joy to all who see the rising sign of your star.
Amen.

Commissioning

Go in faith into this week of Advent.
Go with expectation and gladness towards Christmas Day.

Benediction

And may God the Creator spread joy across the universe,
Christ, the One who is coming, stand waiting to enter
and the Spirit hum the first notes of the celebration.
Amen.

The coming of the unexpected

In this service, alongside the lighting of the Advent candles, there is a symbolic action in response to the word. The symbols for each Sunday are arranged on four tables placed, if possible, at intervals around the outside of the congregation. If you wish, they can be joined by a strip of long purple cloth or ribbon. The symbols for the four Sundays are on the tables and are used as the Sundays come around. The main Advent candles are in the front on the communion table.

Advent 1
Small tea candles on plates placed on all of the four tables so that when they are lit the congregation is surrounded with light.

Advent 2
A large jug of water and bowl into which the water is poured.

Advent 3
A small container of oil for the anointing of the people for healing.

Advent 4
A banner prepared by the congregation ahead of time is hung in the church. This banner holds the handprints of each of the congregation, with their names alongside, made by covering hands with 'finger-paint' (as used in kindergartens) and placing firmly on the cloth and adding names with fabric pen. At the bottom of the banner you may like to add the words 'God is with us. God is within us.'

Opening sentences

Sounds like angel voices of hope,
borne high in the winds of life,
kindnesses earthed on unlikely city streets,
and a clear moment of grace in a person passing by:

All these are heralds of a love yet to come.

Touches of gentle care in the centre of stony harshness,
and insights of wisdom in gatherings of humble people,
ground claimed for justice in deserts of our apathy
and laughter springing true, alongside moments of our tears:
All these are heralds of a love yet to come.
Thanks be to God!

Lighting of the Advent candles

Advent 1
We light this candle
that it may shine around us
reminding us to stay awake
and to expect the coming of the Christ,
the love at the heart of all our longings.

The first Advent candle is lit

Advent 2
Listen for the voice in the desert,
the wisdom from the most unlikely people,
the water of healing and new life in unexpected places,
including within ourselves.

Two Advent candles are lit

Advent 3
For the imprisoned parts of our lives,
healing and risen life are promised.
The signs and gifts will be there,
the unexpected and gentle oil for our anointing
and the messages of reassurance.

Three Advent candles are lit

Advent 4
The life of God is conceived in humankind.
See the fragile light being lit there.

Do not put it away because you cannot understand
where it comes from or where it will take you.
It lies in our hands and is held there in trusting vulnerability.

Four Advent candles are lit

Prayer of confession

O God, it's hard to keep expecting good
when the forces against it seem so great.
It is sometimes difficult to look at the world and believe in love
when we so often experience something other than that.

Silent reflection

O God, we often think we know what life will be
and the boundaries of your possibilities,
boundaries set by people of power,
boundaries set by our own frailty.

Silent reflection

Forgive our lack of faith, O God.
Open our lives and our hearts
to a grander dream for ourselves and for the world.
This we pray in faith.
Amen.

Assurance of pardon

Greater than all our expectations,
wider than all our horizons
stretching forth before us
is the grace and kindness of God.
We are forgiven.
Thanks be to God.

Readings

Use appropriate readings from Year A of the lectionary

Response to the word

Advent 1
Matthew 24.36–44: Stay awake for you do not know the day or the hour

We will now light these other candles,
as signs that our own love for each other
and the love of God surround us as we go,
warming our lives in the waiting.

Candles on the four tables are lit as surrounding light for the congregation

Advent 2
Matthew 3.1–12: John the Baptist in the desert, baptizing with water

Sometimes our lives have felt like a desert,
for years, or a day or a moment.
In the silence, let us remember
the receiving of water for our reviving and restoring,
or when life moved into greater clarity,
like life that is washed clear and which invites a greater wisdom.

A silence is kept

Now I invite anyone who wishes
to come and pour some water from this jug into the bowl,
and either in silence or with a word or phrase
remember the unexpected water for life which you have received.

Advent 3
Matthew 11.2–11: John is in prison and Jesus sends word that the healings are taking place

In the wounded moments of life,
we wait for healing.
It is offered to us as our prayers rise like the fragrance of love.
Sometimes it is given in kindness,
sometimes in endurance and faith for the future

and sometimes in surprising justice and peace.
The Spirit of our God is upon us,
because God has anointed us . . .
We are to give the people
a garland instead of ashes,
and the oil of gladness instead of mourning.
As we hold the fragrant oil in our hands,
let us be open to deeper healing in our lives.
Anoint the back of your hand with oil
or invite another to do so for you.
As we pass the oil to another,
let us surround that person with our prayers.

Advent 4

Matthew 1.18–25: The story of Mary and Joseph as Jesus is conceived

The journey towards Christmas
is a pathway to an unexpected wonder.
God is conceived in human life.
Our life can hold within it the life of God.
The people gathered in and around this congregation
have put their handprints on this banner
as a sign that we believe this
and that we always wait to find God in each other
and in those we meet.
If you haven't put your handprint on the banner,
feel free to do so now.
Then we will hang the banner
as a symbol of our claiming of the life of God among us.

The people do so and the banner is hung

Prayer of intercession

As we bring our prayers to God,
we add to the light surrounding the world.
Our prayers are an act of faith

which invite us and others to believe
that love is present and love will come
in unexpected ways,
born again in the mystery of God's grace.

In the silence, let us reflect on where love is needed.
Then, when we are ready,
let us offer our prayers for ourselves and others
and light the small candles around us.

The people do so

Join your love with our love, O God.
Open our ears that we may hear the cries of those waiting for love.
Open our eyes that we may see new possibilities around us
and open our lives to a different future,
one lit by justice and compassion, wisdom and peace.
This we pray in faith.
Amen.

Sending out

Walk in hope towards Christmas,
carrying with you in kindness all that needs the blessing of love.

Blessing

And may the Holy God hold all creation in tenderness as it longs
    and waits,
Christ Jesus prepare for the birthing of love
and the Spirit sound in melodies of joyful hope in every place.
Amen.

Watch, wait, hope – Advent 1

Call to worship

Watch, wait, hope!
Even now, the tender leaves of peace
may be growing on the trees of life.
Watch, wait, hope!
For the wonder of new love
may be moving towards its birthing.
The Christ will come.
The Word of God will not fail us.

Keep awake!
For the shadows of our doubts will be lifted
and the singing is sounding in the distance.
The Christ will come.
The Word of God will not fail us.

Prayer of invocation

In the spirit of Advent,
we watch for the signs of that which is to come.
We look for them here in this place,
held within our midst in promises of joy.
Come, gracious Jesus, come.
This we pray in your name.
Amen.

Prayer of confession

Loving God, we know that
we are not always good at watching for your Word.
We sometimes confuse our word with yours
or bow to ideas which seem to our advantage
or which others create to threaten us with your judgement.

Silent reflection

Be patient with our failures, O God.
Be present in our watching, Jesus Christ.

We confess to you that often we would rather not wait
for your Word, O God.
Sometimes we long for instant solutions
to issues which arise in our lives
and refuse to pause and pray and listen for your truth.
Sometimes we are so impatient
that we decide what your Word will look like
before it comes to us.
We create you in our own image
rather than honouring your Godliness.

Silent reflection

Be patient with our failures, O God.
Be present in our watching, Jesus Christ.

Then, O God, we know that hope is often hard to hold.
We become depressed and discouraged
and turn away from steady faithfulness in each moment
instead of holding to your promises.

Silent reflection

Be patient with our failures, O God.
**Be present in our watching, Jesus Christ,
and come to us this day.
Amen.**

Words of assurance

The promises of God are wider than the ocean,
deeper than the earth and higher than the skies.
The grace of Jesus Christ will never fail us.
We are forgiven!
Thanks be to God.

Prayer of thanksgiving

We thank you, O God,
for the clear testimony of Jesus Christ.
We thank you that it rings down the ages,
sounding clear through our confusions
and challenging our doubts and fears.
We thank you for the authority
which lies behind this testimony,
born of passionate life
from its beginning to its risen endings.
Amen.

Readings

Isaiah 64.1–9; Psalm 80.1–7, 17–19; 1 Corinthians 1.3–9;
Mark 13.24–37

Sermon

Response to the word

Even as we begin the waiting and the hoping for the coming
    of the Christ,
let us look for small signs of hope which have been given to us.
In the silence, let us look for them.

A silence is kept

Now, let us share the sign which we have seen
and light these tiny candles in celebration.

The people do so

Prayer of intercession

O God, we know that our prayers
are the signs of our hope in you.
Even as our faith is challenged by many things,
even as we sometimes do not know what to pray,

we come into your presence,
trusting that you will listen and respond to us in love.
These are those who are closest to our hearts this day:

The people pray

Add your prayers to ours, Holy Spirit,
for your wisdom is far beyond our knowing.
Wait with us as we try to understand our part
in the well-being of those who wait for love, O God.
Watch over them as they hope for a world which cares enough to act
with a new justice, compassion and as the agents of freedom.
Give to us here an energy and passion for good change
and a faithfulness so that we never give up,
even when we cannot see the way ahead.
**Grant to us a spirit of adventure, O God,
as we walk towards impossible dreams,
for we know that nothing is impossible for you.
This we pray in your name, Jesus Christ.
Amen.**

Commissioning

Do not delay.
The day of the coming of the Christ is every day.
Let us walk forward in Christ's way.

Benediction

And may the Christ be seen when we look behind us,
the Spirit be found walking ahead within our hopes
and the eyes of God the Creator look with love over all creation.
Amen.

Confessing our sins – Advent 2

——⇒►●◄⇐——

For this service you will need

- *A large glass bowl filled with water*

Call to worship

Enter the waiting in hopefulness
for the Christ will not turn away from us.
Prepare yourself this day with a faith
which carries us towards the presence of God without fear.
For the Christ will come in love,
the Christ will come with grace upon grace.

Turn around and find the surprising presence of kindness,
inviting truth without judgement,
frail as a child and strong as all goodness.
For the Christ will come in love,
the Christ will come with grace upon grace.

Prayer of invocation

Draw near to us, O God, in the power of your Holy Spirit.
Be revealed in your holiness this day,
yet safe for us to approach in faith.
Rise within our gathered company
and show us who we are in gentleness.
We pray in your name, O Christ.
Amen.

Prayer of confession

Today we remember that we are called to confess who we are
and to repent as we prepare to receive the coming Christ.

Confessing our sins

We place this bowl of tears on the communion table
as a sign of our grieving as we make our confession.

The bowl is placed

O God, we never come into your presence
without being more starkly aware of who we are.
And yet we come in confidence and in honesty,
knowing that, if we will do that,
we may claim the place which you offer to us every day,
the one close to your love for us.

Silent reflection

We are sorry for the times
when we do not trust your love,
when we are harder on ourselves than you would ever be,
paralysing our lives with unforgiven failures,
anxious about our questions and complexities
or simply unable to face who we are at that moment.

Silent reflection

Forgive us, loving Jesus.
Gather us into your grace again, we pray.

We know that there are times when we judge others,
using your good name to punish people,
offering them less grace than you give to us.
Forgive us, loving Jesus.
Gather us into your grace again, we pray.
Grant to us faith in bringing you our truth each day.
Amen.

Words of assurance

Come to the Christ in openness.
Do not be afraid, because we are never condemned.
Receive the forgiveness of God.
Rise up and live in freedom!
Thanks be to God.

Prayer of thanksgiving

As we move into this time of waiting and reflection,
we praise you, O God,
for we believe that we may do that without fear.
We thank you that we can be ourselves
and still loved and guided by you.
We thank you that you trust people like us
with your mission and ministry in the world
and we pray that we will honour that trust.
Amen.

Readings

Isaiah 40.1–11; Psalm 85.1–2, 8–13; 2 Peter 3.8–15a; Mark 1.1–8

Sermon

Prayer of intercession

Blessings and honour to you, O God,
who brings us into truth
in ways which invite the genuine community
of all humankind and the whole creation.
Thank you that you so love us that you ask
grander and greater things of us
in the adventure of faith.
It is in that strong spirit that we bring you our prayers
as we try to join your dreams
and to carry your cross of brave love towards our neighbours.
These are those who move our hearts in concern today, O God:

The people pray

Be with these people, O God.
Hear our prayers, loving Christ,
and make your hopes alive in all that we do.
Be our wise companion, Holy Spirit,
as we draw near to the struggling places of this earth
and inspire in us a prophetic view of this time in history.

Speak in healing and kindness into our own lives, Jesus Christ,
entering the empty spaces or the closed doors of our souls
and giving us new meaning and purpose in all that we are and do.
In the silence, we bring our personal lives to you,
praying that we will know more clearly
what it is that we need for this day.

A silence is kept

Hear our prayers, O God.
This we pray as we strive to be your true people.
Amen.

Commissioning

Go from here as those who are not afraid to be the humble people
of God,
inviting in our own confessing life, the faith of others in the love
of God.

Benediction

And may the whole earth be restored to hope,
the heavens sing aloud with the promise of good to come
and God in Three Persons, the Holy Trinity, be with us in each
moment.
Amen.

Rejoice – Advent 3

Call to worship

Sing songs of hope into the waiting air
and begin the dance of joy,
for the life of faith is before us.
Look into the distance and see the rising dawn

with shining rays like acts of love
and warming brightness from the heart of God.
**Let us sing praises to God
and watch for the Christ,
for in the longing of Advent
lies the promise of a good which is yet to come.**

Prayer of invocation

Be known to us now, Holy Spirit.
Come and enlarge our faith so that we may watch and wait
    in hope.
Show to us your life which is present in the silences.
Show to us your mind and speak into the emptiness.
Come, gracious Spirit, come.

Prayer of confession

O God, it is sometimes in the centre of the waiting
that we lose hold of hope,
when we have moved past the enthusiasm of our beginnings
but are not yet near enough to see your gifts to us.
We long for quicker answers
and find ourselves impatient to know your will
and to see your face more clearly.

Silent reflection

Be with us in our anxieties, Jesus Christ.
Take our hands and lead us towards your grace.

O God, sometimes we discover small beginnings
of your work in us,
seeds of new life which call us on to greater things
and we let that die in us because we are afraid;
or we see that happening in others
and we fail to encourage them
in case they may bring changes which we do not want
or because we fear for them as they take new steps in life.

Silent reflection

Be with us in our anxieties, Jesus Christ.
Take our hands and lead us towards your grace.
Forgive us and restore us to your way, we pray.
Amen.

Words of assurance

God is faithful to us for ever.
The Christ will visit us with renewing kindness.
We are forgiven.
Thanks be to God.

Prayer of thanksgiving

We give thanks to you, O God,
that day after day, year after year,
we can have absolute confidence
in your love for us
and in your understanding of our journey.
We thank you for the moments
when we find that faithfulness in other people,
in those who have become your good servants.
Thanks be to you, O God.
Amen.

Readings

Isaiah 61.1–4, 8–11; Psalm 126 or Luke 1.47–55; 1 Thessalonians
5.16–24; John 1.6–8, 19–28

Sermon

Prayer of intercession

Loving God, we dare not sing a glad song this day
without bringing before you those here and in other places
for whom singing a song of joy

is a costly and hard-won moment of hope.
Even our own songs of faith
sometimes arise from small moments of delight
in the midst of struggling life.

Silent reflection

We come to you now with our prayers for ourselves and others:

The people pray

Hear our prayers, O God of hope:
Take the ashes of burnt-out life
and the fragments of frail futures
and cover them with the flowers
of your creative possibilities.
Take the tears of the world
and transform our weeping with the oil
which burns with warmth and light for a new day.
Lift our hearts with your encouragement and strength
so that we enter this week
filled with your inspiration for a different future.
For you are the source of our hope,
you are the wonder at the end of the waiting
and you are the God of all eternity.
Amen.

Commissioning

Go now.
The Christ is near and soon we will hear the sounds of joy.
Go in peace.

Benediction

And may the whole earth be renewed in its God,
the universe sound with Christ's promise of coming life
and the Spirit surround us with a cloud of grace.
Amen.

Nothing is impossible – Advent 4

Call to worship

Let the world hold its breath,
for good is coming in all its vulnerable newness.
Deep within our life a wonder is conceived,
hidden in humanity's moments of faithfulness.
Look for it, for it is near.
Believe in it, for it is of God.
Be ready to nurture its life among us,
for it is a precious gift for all history.
Christmas is drawing close.
Thanks and praise be to our God.

Prayer of invocation

As we open our lives to you, this day, Holy Spirit,
we pray that we will know you truly,
recognizing your peace and wisdom deep within our lives,
and responding to your beginnings of good.
Come, Holy Spirit.
Be known to us this day, for we come to you in faith.
Amen.

Prayer of confession

O God, we are not at all sure
that we would have the faith of your people of so long ago –
Mary's openness to your conceiving of the Divine within her,
the trust of Joseph in the face of disturbing realities
and the life within barrenness cherished by Elizabeth.

Silent reflection

Be gentle with us, O God.
Begin a new song of life within us, Jesus Christ.

We confess that sometimes the life
which you conceive among us is a challenge to us,
calling us down pathways which we find hard to tread,
and inviting in us a quality of faith
which carries us well beyond where we have been.
Sometimes it asks of us a confidence in others
which we haven't been prepared to give before
and we are tempted to discourage their hopes.

Silent reflection

Be gentle with us, O God.
Begin a new song of life within us, Jesus Christ,
and gather us into the sweet melody of your forgiveness.
This we pray in your name.
Amen.

Words of assurance

Just as Christ has come in miraculous life
to those who trusted so long ago,
so that Christ comes to us in mercy and love.
We are forgiven.
Thanks be to God.

Prayer of thanksgiving

We thank you, O God,
that we may expect miracles of life beyond our dreaming.
We thank you for the powerful witness
which comes to us in Joseph, Mary and Elizabeth
and for the fact that their lives challenge our own.
We thank you for the journey towards Christmas Day,
the journey of hope and wonder.
Thanks be to you, O God.
Amen.

Readings

Luke 1.26–38; 2 Samuel 7.1–11, 16; Psalm 89.1–4, 19–26; Romans 16.25–27

Sermon

Offering

Response to the word

Before we bring our prayers of intercession,
in the silence, let us acknowledge
those things which we see as impossible –
situations which test our faith to the limits.

A silence is kept

Pray for us, Holy Spirit,
because we cannot find the faith or the words
to bring these our anxious prayers to you.
We know that you will understand our doubts and fears.
Amen.

Prayer of intercession

O God, sometimes when we pray for others and ourselves,
we know that we are praying for what seems impossible to us.
If our prayers are limited by our human visions for the future,
enlarge them with your grandeur of purpose.
If they are limited by our lack of faith,
expand our hearts and souls this day,
that we may dare to pray for nothing less than
the coming of your reign in all the earth.

Silent reflection

In the silence, our lives are touched by you, Jesus Christ.
We will receive all that you offer to us, O God,
all that inspires and opens us to the breadth of your dreams.

In this spirit, we now bring you our prayers for ourselves and others:

The people pray

Break into our lives, O God.
Bring down your justice like rain upon the earth.
Raise up, from within the depths of our lives,
love that will never let our neighbours go.
Cover us with healing grace
and conceive in the centre of despair
surprising freshness and energies for creative change.
Surround us with ideas which spring up
like green shoots in concrete,
defying dryness and challenging deathliness.
For you are our God
and we will be your people.
We would be those who never lay down
the great hope to which we are called.
Amen.

Commissioning

Go and bear witness to the God who confronts all barriers to
    good.
Go in peace and courage.

Benediction

And may the stones under our feet shout aloud the name of
    the Christ,
the skies above send rays of friendly warmth
and the Holy Spirit call to us in each moment.
Amen.

CHRISTMAS

The dawn has come,
gentle as the being of a child,
clothed in the light of its newness.
The dawn has come,
not in the harsh midday sun,
but as fragile rays of pale light,
feeling their way through the darkness.
The dawn has come,
calling the world into vulnerable hope
and claiming a space for God
deep in the centre of our brokenness.
The dawn has come!

The dawning of new life – Christmas Day

➤●◄

Call to worship

The dawn has come,
gentle as the being of a child,
clothed in the light of its newness.
The dawn has come,
not in the harsh midday sun,
but as fragile rays of pale light,
feeling their way through the darkness.
The dawn has come,
calling the world into vulnerable hope
and claiming a space for God
deep in the centre of our brokenness.
The dawn has come!
Let us worship our God,
for this is Christmas Day.

Prayer of invocation

Come, Jesus Christ, come in the wonder of your birthing
along the divine pathway
and into the toughest realities of human life.
Come, Child of God,
and meet the child within each one of us,
gathering us into the loved community of your people,
all people, even us.
Amen.

Prayer of confession

Loving God, who gives us the gift of your Holy Child,
save us from glossing over this day with familiar celebrations,
with often-sung songs and romantic stories.
It is tempting for us to turn your coming
into another form of Christmas decoration, Jesus Christ,
rather than searching for its deeper meaning
and discovering that your birth offers us
our own re-birthing in hope.

Silent reflection

Forgive us, gentle Jesus.
**Open our hearts to the grandest gifts which you bring,
that we may bring our gifts to you in faith.**

If we are tempted to claim this day as our own,
failing to see that you always come in grace
to offer love and peace to all the world
and good news to all humankind:

Silent reflection

Forgive us, gentle Jesus.
**Open our hearts to the grandest gifts which you bring,
that we may bring our gifts to you in faith.**

If we make this day a triumphant celebration
and fail to see how fragile is your coming,
what a small Child of love we hold for nurturing
in the sustaining of your human and Godly life among us:

Silent reflection

Forgive us, gentle Jesus.
**Open our hearts to the grandest gifts which you bring,
that we may bring our gifts to you in faith.
Amen.**

Words of assurance

Have no fear, the Christ has come.
All creation bears witness to the melodies of hope
which spring forth from this humble, human home
which embraces the miracle of our God.
The star of grace hangs over Bethlehem and all the world.
We are forgiven.
Thanks be to God.

Prayer of thanksgiving

We give thanks, O God,
that this day brings joy to so many people,
that, whether they are people of faith or not,
they long to touch the edges of the spirit of Christmas Day.
We thank you that, in small human ways,
so many people try to pause and honour their love for others
with generosity.
We celebrate their longing to give to each other
and to find glimpses of joy in human life.
We thank you, O God,
for the far-reaching wonder of Christmas.
Amen.

Readings

Isaiah 62.6–12; Psalm 97; Hebrews 1.1–4; Luke 2.8–20

Sermon

Prayer of intercession

O God, on this day of all days, we pray for the world,
in its yearning for signs of good and hope,
in its fears that nothing will ever change enough
for free and just life to be given to its people.

Silent reflection

We pray for those who look with longing eyes
for any tiny sign that there are better things to come,
who clutch the fragments of survival
as though tomorrow they may never see the dawn.
Especially we pray for these people and situations:

The people pray

Come in new possibilities among them, Jesus Christ.
As we celebrate your coming
in gifts and gatherings of plenty,
we make our commitment to them,
the commitment that we will not forget them
on this day or the next.

And at this time when, for many people,
betrayals and loneliness become stark,
like the bare bones of death
confronting the fullness of life
as they see those who enjoy the privilege of love,
we pray that you will hold them close to your heart.
Be with all those who find Christmas Day a mockery
and a painful reminder of who they are and what their life is like.
Join us in every place, Jesus Christ.
Visit us whoever we are and wherever we are on this day,
we pray in your name.
Amen.

Commissioning

Go into the world which God so loves
and carry the Good News that the Christ has come to all people.

Benediction

And may the echoes of the angel songs be all around us,
the wisdom of those who followed the star be our guide
and the joyful wonder of those who found the Christ be in
    our hearts.
Amen.

The Christs is here!

⇒➤◦◂⇐

Call to worship

The flame of God's life is lit again,
small spark of childlike hope,
born among the straw and struggles of the world,
held in fragile mangers of love's sanctuaries
and reaching out innocent hands towards cynicism.
The simplicity of God's life
lays itself on the ground among us,
daringly confronting fine theories and dogmas,
small and vulnerable in the midst of worldly power.
The day has come!
The Christ is here.
Let us sing our glad songs of welcome.

Prayer of invocation

Show us the humanness of your face, God with us.
Show us the birthing of your life in this place.
Reach us in this hour with the sounds of angel voices
and shine above us the star which guides the wise.
Come, Child Jesus, come.
Amen.

Prayer of confession

If our minds are so set in knowing
that we fail to feel the wonder and the mystery,
if our hearts are so used to closing their doors to the pain of
    the world
that we dare not open them for fear of what might be expected of us,

44

or if our souls are so centred on the heights of heaven
that we miss the birthing of your life in ordinary places:
Forgive us, Jesus Christ,
and break open the beauty of this day before us, we pray.

If we cannot believe that your gift to us can survive beyond this day,
if we do not see small signs of hope in the world outside this place,
or if life goes on as though Christmas is mostly for children:
Forgive us, Jesus Christ,
and break open the beauty of this day before us, we pray.

If life has lost its capacity to be childlike,
rarely becoming vulnerable and less often open to trust:
Forgive us, Jesus Christ,
and break open the beauty of this day before us, we pray.
For we would share in the wonder of your grace.
Amen.

Words of assurance

The face of the Child of God looks on all the world with kindness,
hopeful for good, giving grace to each and to all,
for this is the time of the re-entry of love.
We are forgiven.
Thanks be to you, O Christ.

Prayer of thanksgiving

Thanks be to God
for the rustling of angel wings close to the grieving.
Thanks for the skies lit up with hope
arching over a groaning creation.
Thanks for the sight of the face of a child
in excited anticipation of good things.
All these remind us of your coming, O Christ.
All these call us away from discouragement
and into the open future of your reign, O God.
Thanks be to you.
Amen.

Readings

Isaiah 62.6–12; Psalm 97; Timothy 3.4–7; Luke 2.(1–7), 8–20

Sermon

Prayer of intercession

Come, O Christ, come into every place where you are needed
   today.
Come among those who believe that they are worth little,
who would not believe that the love of God could be beside them.
Come to those whose lives are so struggling
that they cannot afford to stop and listen for sounds of joy.
Come to those whose Christmas has been so full of busyness
that they have lost sight of its gentleness and wonder.

Silent reflection

Bring into the world the full beauty of your life, Jesus Christ.
Embed yourself among the ordinary days of our human journeys
in ways which reassure us that you are here with us for ever,
touching our lives with depths of understanding.
Come, Child of God, and give to us your hope and peace.

Come to us here in this your church.
Give to us a spirit of childlike delight as we look at the world
   around us.
Inspire in us celebrations of small gifts of love
as we receive from those from whom we never expected to receive.
Come, Child of God, and give to us your hope and peace.
Be our royal Child, clad in newness and grace.
Amen.

Commissioning

Go refreshed in love by another Christmas Day.
Go into a world which has often lost its joy
and bring to it the melodies of God's heaven and earth.

Benediction

Go with the blessing of the Christ who surprises us with grace.
Go with the beauty of the Creator who makes all things new
and go with the Holy Spirit, the bringer of peace.
Amen.

The light shines in the darkness

Call to worship

From the east to the west,
flowing towards all people on earth,
comes the gentle light of hope,
born in the Christchild.
Watch, and see the wonder of the gift.

The life of God lies in vulnerability among us,
spreading grace upon grace across a struggling world,
defying our cynicism
like a budding flower of joy after the fires
or the triumph of a surviving seed in the depth of the coldness.
Watch, and see the wonder of the gift,
for this is Christmas Day.

Prayer of invocation

Come into our lives, gentle Jesus,
surprise us with your kindness and truth,
remind us of our shared vulnerability with you
and of the promise which lies in this day, of all days.
Come, Child of God, come.
Amen.

Prayer of confession

O God, if we approach this day
with more thoughts about our busy preparations
than your gift of peace:
Forgive us and set us free.

If we view Christmas as an ordinary ritual for every year
or one which is mostly about a beautiful story for children:
Forgive us and set us free.

When we experience alienation at this time,
separated from the true celebration by pain or betrayal,
but unwilling to honour that and place it in your loving hands,
stay with us in love, Jesus Christ.

Silent reflection

If we hold this day close to us
and forget those for whom Christmas
is a challenge or a time of suffering:
Forgive us and set us free.
Gather us near to your birthing
and remind us of the depths of its meaning.
This we pray in faith.
Amen.

Words of assurance

The love of Christ surrounds us with warmth and grace.
From the midst of human life,
the understanding of God reaches out towards us.
We are forgiven.
Thanks be to God.

Prayer of thanksgiving

Our hearts are filled with delight, O God,
as we celebrate the joy of this day.
In the face of all that seems to prevail,

we sing songs of hope
and announce the signs of your coming.
We are glad that we are called
to look again at the world with new eyes –
with the expectancy that good is possible,
that love will be among us
and peace is not far away.
Thanks be to you, O Christ.
Amen.

Readings

Isaiah 52.7–10; Psalm 98; Hebrews 1.1–4 (5–12); John 1.1–14

Sermon

Prayer of intercession

On this day, when we celebrate your coming, Jesus Christ,
we pray to you with hope in our hearts.
Even as we pray, we claim again
that you are not distant from our life,
but know it from within
and yet hold out the promise of love and peace for all.
On this day of joy for us,
we pray for those whose life is clouded,
separated from the light of your living
by injustice and oppression, grief, loss or pain:

The people pray

Hold our prayers near to you, Jesus Christ.
Come into the midst of these lives, we pray.
Stand beside them in facing all that brings them despair,
hover over them like an angel song
and bring them sounds of a different future.
Reveal to them wise ones who approach and bear loving gifts.

Then visit us with all that is held dear in Christmas Day:
the lifting up of the holy in the centre of the ordinary,
and the unexpected company of the Christ
as people watch and wait for other things;
the courage and nurturing which may lie in humankind
which is just enough to hold your life among us
in its vulnerability and goodness.
Be known here this day, Jesus Christ.
This we pray in faith.
Amen.

Commissioning

Go with songs of love and hope
to bear witness to all that we have heard and seen.

Benediction

And may the Child of Bethlehem be born into our life,
sheltered by brave love found here
and sustained by faith which will never turn God away.
Amen.

LENT

Journeying in earthliness writ large,
living deeply within our honest searchings,
immersed in the rawness of our temptations:
the Christ holds the faith in fragile arms.
Standing in the wilderness,
surrounded by our toughest questions
and human in every struggling way:
the Christ walks with life wide open ahead of us,
truly human, truly God,
trustworthy in life and trustworthy in death.

With lives wide open
in the wilderness – Lent 1

For this service you will need

- *A long purple cloth flowing from the communion table towards the congregation like a pathway*
- *A basket of varied stones*

Opening sentences

Journeying in earthliness writ large,
living deeply within our honest searchings,
immersed in the rawness of our temptations:
The Christ holds the faith in fragile arms.

Standing in the wilderness,
surrounded by our toughest questions
and human in every struggling way:
The Christ walks with life wide open ahead of us,
truly human, truly God,
trustworthy in life and trustworthy in death.

Prayer of invocation

Wonder of wonders!
God is to be found within our wildernesses,
deep in the centre of our harshest places
and placing a caring hand under all our questions.
Be known to us here, O God, whether we are on firm ground
or the treacherous sands of indecision.
Come, gracious Jesus, come.
Amen.

With lives wide open in the wilderness

Lighting of the candle

Prayer of confession

O Jesus, as we listen to the story of your temptations,
we realize that we are hearing something like your confessions,
the struggles that lay within your earthly life.
Even though you unswervingly chose for good and truth,
we know that you will believe us
when we share how hard it is to choose that way.
In the silence of our own wilderness,
we know who we are and what challenges our life:

Silent reflection

Forgive us, O God,
when we would rather not pause and stay with
all that lies in the shadowy wilderness of our lives,
preferring to press on and leave things for another day.

Silent reflection

Forgive us, O God.
Call us away from this temptation.

If we hold endlessly into grappling with our questions
because we do not want to hear the answers:
Forgive us, O God.
**Sound your truth strongly into our hearts
in the voice of one who knows us well.
Amen.**

Words of assurance

There is no wilderness in life which is out of bounds for God.
In Christ, we are for ever joined with a grace
which comes from earthly experience.
We are forgiven.
Thanks be to God.

Reading

Matthew 4.1–11

Sermon

Response to the word

Let us each take one of these stones,
stones like those under our feet
as we stand in the wilderness places in our lives.

The stones are passed around

Hold the stone and think about things which lie hidden
in the darker parts of your life.
When you are ready, place your stone in silence
within the Lenten space which flows from the cross
or keep it as a sign of your preparedness to reflect on what lies there.

The people do so

Prayer of intercession

Visit us now in the centre of the wilderness of our life, O Christ.
Hold firm among our frail holding to truth,
stand tall when we would lower our life's aspirations,
speak boldly into our false assumptions
and look us in the eye when we fool ourselves
by pretending to be doing your will.

Silent reflection

Make transparent the wiles of those who would tempt us,
calling to us in voices of sweetness and reason
while attempting to capture our very souls.

Silent reflection

Be with all those today
who need your company in the wilderness of their lives.
Especially we remember these people and situations:

The people pray

Remind us, O Christ, of your true way.
Go with us along the path of humility,
in the spreading of good and justice and compassion into the world,
in offering love which is not founded on our own gain
and in finding peace which is beyond describing.
This we pray in trembling faith.
Amen.

Offering

Commissioning

The world is often found by passing through the wilderness.
Go in courage because Christ has walked that way before us.

Benediction

May truth shine as a star in the night sky,
righteousness shout its freedom into the centre of our confusions
and God be in our beginning, our centre and our endings.
Amen.

With lives wide open
to being reborn – Lent 2

For this service you will need

- *A long purple cloth flowing from the communion table towards*
  the congregation like a pathway
- *A small unopened flower bud*

Opening sentences

The Body of Christ is the womb-space of love,
conceiving new life day by day,
holding us in unconditional grace
until we are ready to be born afresh,
and carrying the labour and bleeding of our birthing
in an energy of kindness
which stands forever waiting for us.
This is our God.
This is the Christ.

From the earth the songs of praise arise,
from the skies the rains of greening gently fall
and our lives pause in awe as we lift our hearts this day.

Prayer of invocation

Be found walking with us in this hour, O God,
wise company as we wonder about our lives and your truth.
Be our inspiration as we contemplate the next days
and the one who never condemns us in our questioning and frailty.
Be with us now, Holy Spirit of Christ, Holy Spirit of God.
Amen.

Lighting of the candle

Prayer of confession

O God, there are times when we sink with relief
into old decisions about faith,
living out of past times when we agreed to love you
and shielding ourselves from further challenges.

Silent reflection

Take our hand, Jesus Christ.
Look into our hearts and search us out,
then forgive us for our reluctance to walk further into your life.

With lives wide open to being reborn

Sometimes we hold our place as your people
with unwarranted pride,
pointing with triumph to a moment of commitment
instead of living in gratitude for the ongoing grace we receive.

Silent reflection

Take our hand, Jesus Christ.
**Look into our hearts and search us out,
then forgive us for our reluctance to walk further into your life.**

If we are resisting your voice within us and around us
which invites us to be born again into newer life,
to enter your Body for a time of cherishing
which will ready us for a different emerging and growing:
**Take our hand, Jesus Christ.
Look into our hearts and search us out,
then forgive us for our reluctance to walk further into your life.
This we pray in faith.
Amen.**

Words of assurance

The offer of God always stands ahead of our life.
We may be born again,
leaving behind all that is of death or guilt.
We are not condemned.
We are forgiven.
Thanks be to God.

Reading

John 3.1–17

Sermon

Response to the word

To be born again
is to be prepared to enter the womb of God's love
as though our lives are reconceived.
I will place this unopened bud within the circle of cloth,

the cloth which touches the cross,
the sign of the cost which the Christ is prepared to pay
that we may live.

The bud is placed

In the silence, I invite you to imagine
that you place your life within the circle of God's love
and wait for a new understanding of who you are
and who you could be.

A silence is kept

Hold us, Jesus Christ,
recreate us, God who is our Loving Parent,
and set us free to live, Holy Spirit.
Amen.

Prayer of intercession

We pray today, O God,
for all who cannot imagine receiving life
beyond that which they now live.
We pray for those who are closed in by need and injustice,
or bowed down by illness or anxiety:

The people pray

Walk with them, Jesus Christ,
offering them your love,
healing their wounds and living within their questions.
Raise in us such passionate life
that we share in the bringing of new life to others.

May we so live that the testimony of our journey with you
speaks to others in joy and hope.
May compassion and courage blossom in us
so that all people of goodwill long to join that way of life,
and may our faith be renewed every day
so that the world may never give up its dream for a greater good.

May the whole creation echo the promise
of the endless rebirthing of love.
Amen.

Offering

Commissioning

Go forth into the world as those who are born again
into the life of God.

Benediction

Go in brave hope as those who are loved of God,
forgiven in the power of the Spirit
and accompanied by Christ in life's every journey.
Amen.

*With lives wide open
to the living water of Christ – Lent 3*

For this liturgy you will need

- *A large jug of water*
- *A clear glass bowl*

Opening sentences

God's deep heart of life
is like a well of infinite love.
It flows towards all creation
in living waters of grace.
Praise be to God.

Christ sits beside our life,
inviting us to open ourselves,
body, mind, heart and soul

to the flowing newness of eternal life.
Praise be to God.
Let us rejoice in hope.

Prayer of invocation

Be known to us in this place
and wherever we pause to be near to you, O Christ.
Take us by surprise if we cannot believe that you would visit us.
Meet us wherever you will so that we may receive
the wonder of your living water for this day and all that lies ahead.
This we pray in your name.
Amen.

Prayer of confession

O God, forgive us if we underestimate your love.
When we confine it to certain people and places,
and when we fail to recognize it in our own midst,
shock us out of our assumptions and narrow views of you,
    we pray.

Silent reflection

If we cannot imagine that you would ask us for water
to refresh your life in the world, Jesus Christ,
open our eyes to the places where you sit and wait.

Silent reflection

When we reap without sowing
and feel no gratitude for those who have gone before,
or sow your seeds of life
and become discouraged when we cannot see the harvest,
remind us of your free gifts for our life
and forgive us for our lack of generosity, O Christ.
For we are your very human people
and we need your grace.
Amen.

Words of assurance

The living water from the life of God flows over all people in love.
It pours forth when we have not deserved it,
it sprinkles in coolness over the heat of our anxieties
and calms our troubled hearts.
We are forgiven as a free gift of grace.
Thanks be to God.

Reading

John 4.6–42

Sermon

Response to the word

Here is the water which reminds us of Christ's offer to us all.

The jug of water is lifted high

In this moment, I invite you to pause in your life
and ask yourself whether you are prepared to receive
the living water which Christ offers to you
for the refreshing of your life.
In the silence, feel for the parts of your life which are dry
or dying for want of loving nurture.

A silence is kept

As I pour this water into the bowl,
hold your life open to receive the renewing of God.

The water is poured and a brief silence is kept

Bless and keep us, O God,
for our lives are barren without you.
Amen.

Prayer of intercession

Flow the living waters of your creative life
around us, among us and within us, O God.

Help us to draw from your gift
and to make a faithful commitment to share it with others,
filling up the empty cups around us
with overflowing rivers which carry with them
the waters of change towards the world which you planned.
Give us a new vision of a world
in which people trust the kindness of others,
in which leaders are not corrupted by power,
in which violence does not prevail
nor lies hold the world to ransom
as the poor lie dying and needy before us.

Silent reflection

Be near to us, Jesus Christ.
**Flow your living water over us, O God,
that our hearts and hands may be made clean,
and that our lives may arise in freshness
to inspire all around us with hope that things can be changed.**

Hold close to you these people and situations for which we
now pray:

The people pray

Guide them close to the wells of your nourishment, O God,
and the springs of living water
which will lift up their lives in energy and courage.
**These prayers we pray in your name, O Christ.
Amen.**

Commissioning

Let us go to walk the way of faith
and discover the Christ waiting for us there with the water of life.

Benediction

And may the wells of God's life be found beside the road,
Christ Jesus meet us in unexpected places
and the Spirit be with us on every hill and in every valley.
Amen.

With lives wide open
to the gift of healing – Lent 4

——➤◦◄——

For this service you will need

- *A small bowl of fragrant oil*

Opening sentences

God is mystery and awe,
God is Spirit and truth,
God is grand Creator and Holy Christ.
And one thing we know:
in the moment of love,
in the gift of healing,
in the act of grace,
in the holding to hope
our God is with us.

Prayer of invocation

Be our God now, Creator, Christ and Holy Spirit.
Touch the place which you once touched in your people
and remind us again of the gift of your presence with us and
    within us.
Be real to us in this moment, that we may be gathered up in love.
Amen.

Prayer of confession

There are times, O God,
when we forget we ever knew you.
We enter an empty space or a dark night of the soul
and you seem absent from us.
We forget the past experiences of your love

and feel that you have left us.
Our hearts are filled with doubt
and the future looks lonely
as we grapple with our lives and their questions and traumas.
Sometimes it is as if our lives sit alone in the universe
and we cannot find our way back to you and to the care of others.

Silent reflection

Come, Holy Spirit, come.
**Remind us of your grace, loving Jesus,
and forgive us when we choose to live distant from you.**

If we are given words of hope by others,
stories of their life with you that have transformed them,
but we do not trust this good news
and discourage them from their radiant joy,
or if we push away small gifts
which you offer to us as your company
in a tough part of life
because we insist on a larger miracle:
**Come, Holy Spirit, come.
Remind us of your grace, loving Jesus,
and forgive us when we choose to live distant from you.
Return us to faith
and enlarge our hope, O God.
Amen.**

Words of assurance

Our God is the God who seeks us out,
who discovers our closed eyes,
opens them and leads us towards grace.
Even in our frailty of faith,
we are forgiven and brought home to God.
Amen.

Reading

John 9.1–41

Sermon

Response to the word

God's healing takes many forms.
Only God knows what lies within our life waiting for healing.
The healing may come in unexpected ways.
When we pray for healing,
the promise is that, after we have asked, searched
and knocked on the door of God's love,
the Holy Spirit will be sent to us.
Let us pass around this bowl of fragrant oil,
the sign of the anointing of God's love in each life.
Hold the bowl for a moment as you reflect
on what needs healing in your life.
If you wish to anoint your hand or forehead with oil,
feel free to do so.

The bowl is passed

Pour your healing life upon us, Holy Spirit.
This we pray in Christ's name.
Amen.

Prayer of intercession

Dear God, bearer of miraculous life,
we know that there are people in numbers too great to count
who wait each day for their lives to be changed.
They wait for gifts of healing, or even basic health care,
which would be like a miracle in their lives.
They wait for enough food to feed their children,
or a day when they could enjoy the food
which we take for granted.
They wait for an end to violence and abuse,
for the chance that they might wake up without fear.
They wait for opportunities in life
which would make each day a delight rather than endless labour.

Silent reflection

We pray for all these people, O God,
and for others whose voices are rarely heard.

The people pray

And now we pray for ourselves, O God.
Create in us many miracles, O God.

Heal us from apathy and indifference,
and from cynicism and refusals to believe
that we could be part of the bringing in of just changes.
Create in us many miracles, O God.

Raise up in us prophetic witnesses to your love,
and those who bring testimonies to the grandeur of your gifts.
Create in us many miracles, O God,
that we ourselves may see and believe in the hope of your reign.
Amen.

Commissioning

Let us go out from this place
and tell the people what God has done for us.

Benediction

And may the miracles of God spread across the world
in gifts of faith, endurance, shared love, healing and forgiveness,
announcing the wonder of transforming possibilities for all people.
Amen.

With lives wide open
to the gift of life – Lent 5

For this service you will need

- *Main Christ candle on communion table*
- *Tapers and small candles either on the table or on a purple cloth
  draped from the table on to the floor*

Call to worship

God whose life holds all life,
God for whom death is not the end,
God of all time and every place:
We gather here before you in faith.

Christ with the human feet,
treading along every road in every rocky place,
forming the way as you go
so that we may see you ahead of us:
We gather here before you in faith.

Spirit marked with all the signs of heaven,
healing, comforting, enduring and liberating:
We gather here before you in faith.
Let us worship our God.

Lighting of candle

Prayer of invocation

Break through our barriers of unbelief, O God.
Visit us within our hopes and fears today.
Come to us in clear life as we gather here,
that our lives may be renewed through your healing life.
Amen.

Prayer of confession

Holy Jesus, renewer of life,
we know there are times when we do not believe
that you can save us.
We lie down and die to life
before we have held ourselves open to your healing
or any other gifts which you may bring
for giving us fresh hope and courage.

Silent reflection

Forgive our lack of trust, loving Jesus.
Forgive our acceptance of the things of death.

Sometimes we commit others to a form of death
because we cannot imagine what could change
and bring them into new life.
Sometimes we are impatient for solutions
when you are gently leading us
down the hard path towards a different way forward.

Silent reflection

Forgive our lack of trust, loving Jesus.
Forgive our acceptance of the things of death.

Forgive us when we doubt
that, in life or death, you never leave us alone,
that you hold everything in your loving hands,
for us and for those whom we love.
Forgive us if we think that you do not care
when those close to us leave us in death,
or that death is some sort of punishment
and an end of life and love.
Be with us, Jesus Christ, in life and in death.
Amen.

Words of assurance

Death bows before the sacred life of God,
all death and every death.
The refusal to lay down guilt is to hold ourselves into deathly places
by separating ourselves from the love of God's love.
Choose life.
Forgiveness waits for us, if we will receive it.
Thanks be to God.

Prayer of thanksgiving

We thank you, O God,
that there are no boundaries to your love.
We thank you that, even in death,

you travel with us and save us.
We thank you that you join our grieving,
weeping with us for the loss of those we love,
and joining us at the tombs of life.
We thank you for the signs all around us
of life which springs forth after deathly experiences
and for the power of renewal in all creation.
Amen.

Reading

John 11.1–45

Sermon

Response to the word and prayer of intercession

However we understand the story of the raising of Lazarus,
the eternal offer from God to all humankind
is the gift of life which rises in the face of death.
In these next moments,
let us reflect on what parts of our lives
and the life of the world
have died and wait for Christ's gift of life:

Silent reflection

And now I invite you to come forward, if you wish,
and light one of these small candles
as a sign that you ask God for new life
in some part of your journey
or in some part of the life of the world.
Feel free to do that in silence,
or with a sharing in a word or phrase.

The people do so

Come to us, healing God.
Come to us as one who holds us in your arms
when our bodies, minds, hearts or souls
are weak with pain, or ill with the afflictions of humankind.

Come to us like a loving mother,
searching for that which troubles us
and assuring us that you are near.
Come to us like a loving father,
tenderly embracing us with your kindness.
In the silence, we bring all that ails us before you:

A silence is kept

Hear our prayers, O God,
and stay with us if we fear the deaths before us.
As we look at our world,
we see so many people and situations
which seem destined for dying.

Silent reflection

As we look upon these troubled parts of life,
give to us the wisdom and inspiration
which comes from seeing them through your eyes, Jesus Christ.
**Show us the life that could rise from within
what seem to be deathly places, O God.
Grant us new life within ourselves
so that we never give others over to death
when there are your ways through to freedom and hope.
Be with us, we pray, Holy Spirit.
Amen.**

Commissioning

Let us leave this place as those
who have been freed from the bonds of death.

Benediction

Go in peace, go in grace.
Go with the life-renewing power of Jesus Christ
and the everlasting love of God.
Amen.

PALM SUNDAY

The stones cry out in joy,
the trees wave their branches in delight,
the myriad birds burst forth into song
in the city and the countryside.
For the Christ comes riding among the people,
bone of our bone
and flesh of our flesh:
God who chooses to share our life,
we praise and worship you!

The stones cry out

For this service you will need

- *A cross on the communion table*
- *A bowl of stones*

Call to worship

The stones cry out in joy,
the trees wave their branches in delight,
the myriad birds burst forth into song
in the city and the countryside.
For the Christ comes riding among the people,
bone of our bone and flesh of our flesh:
God who chooses to share our life,
we worship you!

Prayer of invocation

Be known within our life today, O God who travels with us.
Open our hearts to receive you.
Open our lips to sing your praises.
Open our souls to the depths of your passion for us
and for all people.

For this is the day when we remember your entry into the city,
into the city of those who have gone before us.
Be with us as you were with them, O God.
Amen.

Prayer of confession

God of grace,
if we are so busy or so anxious

that we do not pause to receive you
when you pass through our life:
Forgive us, O God.

If we are so sure that we will recognize you in your coming
that we refuse to be open to the way others may see you:
Forgive us, O God.

When we choose to turn our faces away so that we do not see you
because that does not fit within our plans:
Forgive us, O God.

If we have lost the joy of discovering your presence,
and are going about our life as though there are few surprises:
Forgive us, O God, and renew our life with you.
Amen.

Words of assurance

Jesus is always travelling towards us,
in all our lostness,
in all our weakness and failures.
This God is never defeated by who we are.
Receive the Christ. Receive the grace that is offered.
We are forgiven!
Thanks be to God.

Prayer of thanksgiving

Thanks be to God, the Humble One,
the One who travels towards all that we fear
and all that overpowers us.
Thanks be to God who invites our love
and moves through the centre of our life
in hope and truth.
Thanks be to God for the times of hope
when the pathway to peace seems to unfold before us.
Amen.

Palm Sunday

Readings

Isaiah 50.4–9a; Psalm 118.1–2, 19–29; Philippians 2.5–11;
Luke 19.28–40

Sermon

Prayer of intercession

O God, we have gathered these stones from our roadside,
the roadside where you will always be found journeying among
    the people
with compassion and determination.
As we bring our prayers to you,
we will place a stone before your cross.

Even as the stones cry out in love for you,
we know they also cry out as you pass for those who suffer.
This stone cries out for those who struggle in poverty:

The people add their prayers and place the stone

This stone cries out for those who suffer in war and violence:

The people add their prayers and place the stone

This stone cries out for those who grieve in loss and loneliness,
    or struggle with illness:

The people add their prayers and place the stone

This stone cries out for your church in this day, O God,
as we try to be faithful:

The people add their prayers and place the stone

This last stone cries out for each one of us,
as we long for the day when we will fully share in your abundant
    life:

The stone is placed

Hear the crying out of the stones as you pass, Jesus Christ,
for in you lies healing and hope,
all that we need for our life.
Amen.

Commissioning

Go in joy for Jesus walks between us.
Go in humble faith,
in all our humanness,
for we will be led by the Spirit.

Benediction

And may the whole creation bear witness to its God,
the earth be a carpet of green for the carrying of the Gospel
and the sun warm every cold place
as the sacred life of the Spirit dreams its dreams for all creation.
Amen.

Growing conviction

For this service you will need

• *Palm branches or branches of a tree which is native to your area*

Call to worship

Blessed is the One who comes in the name of our God!
Hosanna to the Christ, the Messiah!
Praise be to the One who looks upon the suffering of the people
with gentle eyes in a face like flint,
forever steadfast in love and courage,

never turning away from all that would challenge good and truth.
Praise be to you, Jesus Christ!
Let us worship God.

Prayer of invocation

We have prepared this place for your entry, Jesus Christ.
We have gathered here to meet you,
as the people stood by the road to Jerusalem,
hoping to be touched by your life and hope,
growing in conviction that the Messiah is among us.
Be present to us today, Jesus Christ, the One for whom we wait.
Amen.

Prayer of confession

Brave Jesus,
we confess that often we do not have your courage
or your faith and hope.
We falter before the powers of evil,
or grow cynical, pretending that we do not care.
Our hearts fail within us
and we lose hold of our sense of connection with your life,
trying, as best we can, to survive on our own.
Remind us of who we are, Jesus Christ.
Forgive us as we stand here in hope.

Jesus, who loves us as ordinary people,
we confess that we often sing 'Hallelujah' to you one day
and then turn our faces from you on the next.
Sometimes we even have excellent excuses for doing that –
like we need another resolution or another study group
before we can follow you on your way,
or stand cheering for your cause by the road.
Remind us of who we are, Jesus Christ.
Forgive us as we stand here in humble hope.
Forgive us as you did your early friends.
Amen.

Words of assurance

On this day, of all days, we remember that our God
steadfastly goes towards costly death rather than desert us.
On this day, grace is still offered to us all.
We are forgiven.
Praise be to you, Jesus Christ!
Amen.

Prayer of thanksgiving

Dear God, who calls on all sorts of people to prepare
the moments for your entry into our life,
we thank you for your including of us
as you go on your way.
We thank you that you give to us times
when we can stand with you,
even for a little while,
and that you are a God of celebration and joy.
Amen.

Readings

Isaiah 50.4–9a; Psalm 118.1–2, 19–29; Philippians 2.5–11;
Matthew 21.1–11

Sermon

Prayer of intercession

Gracious Jesus, today you challenge us
to see who stands between you and the survival of your life.
You invite us to see who waits to try to destroy
those who are the agents of good
and to have the courage to walk towards them as you did.
In the silence, bring to us your call for courage and insight:

A silence is kept

We remember the people of old
who at least made the way softer for your passing

and we hope that we can join them today.
Give to us a sense of where the road for justice and love
needs cushioning against harshness and
waits for the holding out of supporting hands
against the ruggedness of rocky places.
Call us to be those who make the way safer
for those who dare to tread it for you.

A silence is kept

Lift up within us the celebrating of our old stories,
our moments of brave faith which we have forgotten,
so that we may be encouraged to be who you invite us to be.
Amen.

Commissioning

We are the holders of the palm branches for the Christ!
We are the ones who cheer God on the way.
Let us place our palm branches (or branches from a native tree)
down the aisle of the church as a sign that we are those who will
try to prepare the way for good.

The people do so

Go into the world in celebration and growing conviction.

Benediction

And may Jesus come over the brow of every hill towards us,
flowers and trees spring forth from the Creator along each road
and the Spirit breathe courage into our souls as we go.
Amen.

The cheering on of good

For this service you will need

* *A flowing purple cloth which comes from a cross on the communion table down the aisle towards the congregation*
* *Green branches*
* *A plate or plates with small candles and a taper*

Opening sentences

The Christ of hope enters the city,
riding into our lives in humility
but with all the authority of good.
The Christ comes among us in grace.

The Christ dares to ride towards our life,
inviting our company
and affirming in us every trembling promise.
The Christ comes among us in grace.

Not wearing the garments of power,
but staying in simple open-armed humanity
and welcoming our every moment in the true celebration of life:
The Christ comes among us in costly love.
Let us bring our praises.

Prayer of invocation

Ride into our lives in gentleness, brave Jesus.
Come through the centre of our gathering here
so that we may see in our midst the grand hope of your courage.
Awaken in us echoes of your amazing life,
that we may leave here as different people.
Come, gracious Jesus, come.
Amen.

Prayer of confession

O God, sometimes we hear you inviting us to prepare for a day
when you will be seen in all the world
and we cannot imagine ourselves being part of that.
We confess that we wait in hopes of others
looking for the colt which will carry you.

Silent reflection

Forgive us, living God.
Call us to greet your life as it calls to us this day.

Then, even when we think we see you,
we do not always welcome you, O God.
We stay in the homes of our comfort and complacency
rather than venturing into the streets of life
to find you riding ahead of us
or striding towards the tough struggles for good.

Silent reflection

Forgive us, living God.
Call us to greet your life as it passes by this day.
This we pray.
Amen.

Words of assurance

The life of God will not be denied.
It travels before us and between us in brave clarity.
We are offered full forgiveness in this moment.
Receive it as a truly gracious gift.
Amen.

Prayer of thanksgiving

We thank you, O God,
that there is a moment as we walk towards Good Friday
when we can remember that the people cheered you on.
We thank you that we can pause and join them,
even if we betray you later.

The cheering on of good

Thank you that you give to humankind
gifts of hope about ourselves along the way,
times when we remember who we were
and the beauty of your presence,
as we recognized a holy life
which many of us can see as the source of our hope.
Thanks be to you, O God.
Amen.

Reading

Matthew 21.1–11

Sermon

Response to the word

In response to the word,
let us lay branches along the sides of this cloth
as our commitment to cheer on the good in life,
even if it is only for one moment or one day.

The people do so

Affirmation of faith

And now let us stand and affirm our faith together:
We believe that the welcoming of good
will never stay silent,
that in every age the sounds of celebration
will echo into the air,
as we see what might be in us
and in the world.

We believe that we are those
who will lay the carpets of welcome
for good in us and good in others,
that the Christ will join us in those moments
and love will lift up our hearts.
This we believe.

Prayer of intercession

Living God, there are many places around the world
which long for the strong glad entry of justice and love.
Come into the streets of our cities and towns, we pray.
Ride along them towards all who would oppress.
Gather as you go
all who cannot believe that they could be loved,
who have never been able to stand near to kindness and
    acceptance
or see it travel past, surrounded by applause.
We bring before you our special concerns now:

The people pray and are invited to light candles on the pathway of
celebration as a way of cheering on people towards good and hope

Give us the strength to face all
who would destroy your dream for creation, O God.
Make pathways of your courage for our feet,
lay carpets of green for our greater growing in hope
and sound cheering voices in our ears
as we dare to venture forth in your name.
Go with us, loving Jesus, lead us on, Holy Spirit.
Amen.

Commissioning

Go in faith to welcome all that is of God in the world,
knowing that the Christ is moving before us.

Benediction

And may hosannas of joy sound in all the earth,
welcoming the One who looks evil in the face,
and may the presence of God
lift high all our hopes for the transforming of life.
Amen.

GOOD FRIDAY

See this, our Christ,
standing starkly within the empty spaces
of our nothingness and despair,
embedded deep within the unyielding rocks of our pain,
holding arms wide open to embrace our most guilty life.
See this, our Christ,
Jesus of Good Friday,
Jesus of costly mercy.

The day the world changed

Opening sentences

On that day, the world changed –
dark skies of violence and hate
covered our long-held imaginings of good.
On that day, the world changed –
cold spread abroad in fearful hearts
as though the sun might never rise again.
On that day, the world changed –
and love lay there with life poured out
dead with injustice,
and dead as life became of less worth than power.
On that day, Good Friday,
the world was changed for ever.

Prayer of invocation

Come to us this day in a new way, Jesus Christ.
Come as the one who is not afraid of anything in human life.
Come as the brave Christ who stays in the tombs of our life,
and who walks towards violence and hate
with a soul which shrinks from nothing.
Come and convince us again that, whatever we may fear,
we cannot kill our God.
Amen

Prayer of confession

God who never turns away from us in rejecting judgement,
we enter this day as the one
where we are invited to look deeply into our lives.
Embrace us with your costly love as we face our realities –

the tough truth about ourselves
which stands stark and clear before your cross.

Silent prayer

Loving Jesus, we grieve our constant failure
to be your true people.
Our lives are often limited by our own concerns
and closed off by prejudice and ignorance.

Silent prayer

Show to us our self-righteousness as we tell ourselves
that we are the chosen ones in this world.
Break through our self-deception so that we may see ourselves
as ordinary human beings,
those who share in the crucifying of good
and who are far more dependent on your grace than we will
    ever own.

Silent prayer

Forgive us, O God:
**For we know not what we do
and we know not what we have done.
Amen.**

Words of assurance

The God who hangs before us in suffering and death
is the God who would rather die than stop loving us
and who offers us forgiveness.
As we stand before the grandeur of this love,
let us receive the pardon of the Christ and live as people
who walk in faith towards Easter Day.
Amen.

Prayer of thanksgiving

We thank you, O God,
that you travel with us down the days of life,
entering the places which we dread

and staying in the darkness and emptiness alongside us.
We will never forget your kindness in our every moment,
   loving Jesus.
We thank you on this day, Jesus Christ,
for love which surpasses human knowledge
and grace which bears the pain of death.
Amen.

Readings

Isaiah 52.13—53.12; Psalm 22; Hebrews 10.16–25; John
18.1—19.42

Sermon

Prayer of intercession

On this day, of all days, O God,
we bring to you all the oppressions and suffering in this
   troubled world.
We do this in confidence,
knowing that nothing is too much or too little for you:

The people bring their prayers

Gather up all of these, our prayers,
into the loving healing and costly carrying of pain
which lies within your own Body, Jesus Christ,
that soon all may be changed into new life.
And now we pray that we, as your earthly Body,
may so be transformed and inspired by your love for us,
that we too may absorb into our life the needs and struggles
   of the world
and create there a miracle of grace
and a leading forth into a different day.
In the silence,
we honour all that you have done for us and for all people:

A silence is kept

Give us faith to believe in a love as great as yours, O Christ.
Amen.

Commissioning

Go out in quiet faith
to walk the way towards the hope of Easter Day
and our meeting with the risen Christ.

Benediction

And may we dare to look all deathliness in the face,
and find the love of God waiting there behind it,
calling us to follow down the dark reaches of our life
into the safe arms of Jesus Christ.
Amen.

The torn fabric

For this service you will need

* *A large white sheet for a shroud placed on the floor*
* *A basket of different pieces of fabric*
* *A large cross*

In the emptiness

In the emptiness,
in the fearful spaces,
before the wide shroud which holds our deaths,
we stop in shock and wonder what we have done.
Is it possible that we have killed our God?
Can it be that there is nothing left?

The shroud is placed in the centre

Is there a silence for ever?
Stay in this place and look.
Stay in this place and dare to see.
Stay in this place and wait for a miracle
in the centre of our nothingness.
For, on Good Friday,
the world knew its God.

Covering the emptiness

While we wait,
let us cover the emptiness with the fabric of our lives,
coloured in humanness and variety,
worn thin with our struggles
or grown thick with our defences against pain.
Let us place the fabric of our lives over the spaces,
touching the edges together
like holding on to each other in our ordinary failing life.

The people choose a piece of cloth as an image of the fabric of their lives, and place it on the shroud

The cross

Lift high the cross of Jesus Christ,
then lay it earthed among our lives,
joined with us in the emptiness,
staying deeply among our reality,
touching every truth and daring it to speak,
feeling every dying thing
as it bleeds in hiddenness or shrieks in despair.

The cross is placed upon the fabric of life

Staying with truth

As the cross is embedded in our life
it calls forth the truth:
the truth of life torn asunder,
bleeding in splashes of painful colour,
and hope lying dead with injustice.
It cries out for life lying wounded in failures
and crucified by loss of love.
It stands in silent witness to the truth
of corruptions and of powers which claim
that their own agendas are more valuable than vulnerable lives.
The cross lies there among us
telling us the truth about who we have been
and who we are,
down the centuries of life.

The fabric of our lives is torn and thrown in a heap

Readings

Use the set lectionary readings for Good Friday

Sermon

Prayer

O God, who never turns away from us in shock or repulsion,
we enter this day as the one
where all that we dread in ourselves is gathered together
and placed on your cross.

Silent prayer

Give to us the faith and hope which we need
as we remember what it costs to so love the world
and as we grieve our constant failure to reach that level of love.

Silent prayer

Strip away from us the defences behind which we hide.
Tear away the veils of illusion so that we may see ourselves,

and all people, as eternally human
before the universal grace which is yours.
Forgive us, O God.
Sometimes, like those who crucified you,
we know not what we do.
But often we do know what we have done
and yet we place ourselves before you for forgiveness.
Amen.

The torn fabric of life is placed on the cross

Prayer

We thank you, O God,
for your company in the deathly graves of our life,
the vivid courage of your journey down into all our realities,
the bleeding of your life which mingles with the bleeding of
    our life
and the echoing down the centuries of this love beyond all
    other love.

Gather all of our prayers
into the loving, healing and costly carrying of pain
which lies within your own Body, Jesus Christ.
We thank you, O God, for the saving power
which lies within your greatest vulnerability
and which is offered to us if we will stay in this moment
and wait for truth and grace.

In the silence,
we honour all that you have done for us and for all people:

A silence is kept

Give us faith, O God.
Give us faith to believe in a love as great as yours, Jesus Christ.
Wrap our lives in the cherishing shroud of your grace.
Amen.

The shroud is wrapped around the cross

Dismissal

Let us go out in silent reflection and in the company of the Christ,
who never leaves us, even unto death.
Let us stay with truth and love this day.

Blessing

And may we dare to look all deathliness in the face,
and find the love of God waiting there behind it,
calling us to follow down the dark reaches of our life
and into the safe arms of Jesus Christ.
Amen.

Walking towards the open arms of Jesus

For this service you will need

- *A large cross*
- *Felt 'footsteps', some of which may be made by children to represent their own feet*
- *As people come in they are asked to select a footstep*

Call to worship

There is our God,
with arms spread wide in vulnerability,
embracing the whole of our life
in its every deathly reality.
There is the Christ, our God.

Gathered into those outstretched arms
is all that we are in our humanness,
all our failures and guilty secrets,
all our shame and responsibility
for the wounding of the innocent
in ourselves and in others.
There is the Christ, our God.

Jesus waits for us
with loving arms
and a kind heart.
**There is Jesus
waiting for us to walk forward in faith.**

We join with all of humankind

Addressing the children

Many people walk across the earth.
Even though we cannot see them all,
they leave their footprints on the ground.
Have you seen their footprints in the sand?
We are going to put all these footprints in front of the cross
to remind us that Jesus loves all the people in the world –
indigenous people, people from Asia, the Pacific Ocean, Africa and
Europe, the Middle East and North and South America.
They are all people who Jesus loves and they are our sisters and
    brothers.

The children place extra footprints before the cross

These are the marks left by humankind
in its stumbling, suffering and sometimes celebrating journey.
Some of these footprints are of those who have struggled for
    survival,
some are of those who have joined the Christ in love and justice
and paid the price for that.
Most of them are left by people like us
who fail one day and live in grace on another.

Walking towards the open arms of Jesus

We will walk through the footprints
left by all who have gone before us
and those who walk with us in our day.
For there is no way towards the cross
other than through the lives of the people.

Reading

John 18.1—19.42

Response to the word

In response to the word,
let us dare to walk towards the open arms
and open life of Jesus Christ.
Let us walk through the footprints of humankind,
remembering, as we go, the truth about ourselves
and all the human life that Jesus gathers to himself on this day.

As we place our footprint near to the cross,
let us place ourselves within the saving love which waits for us
there.

The people place their own footprints

A silence is kept followed by chanting or a quiet hymn

Prayers of confession and intercession

O God, we know with grief that we are there in your story.
We, too, betray you when things become hard or costly.

Silent reflection and drumming

For our every betrayal, forgive us, Jesus Christ.
Forgive us and restore our life this day.

We, too, turn our faces away from those suffering injustices.

Silent reflection and drumming

For our every participation in injustice, forgive us, Jesus Christ.
Forgive us and restore our life this day.

Sometimes it is hard to be good.
We make mistakes and we forget who we should be.

Silent reflection and drumming

We are sorry, Jesus Christ.
Forgive us and restore our life this day.

We, too, are part of the violence and abuse suffered by the
    innocent.

Silent reflection

For our every silence in the face of violence to others, forgive us,
    Jesus Christ.
Forgive us and restore our life this day.

Death is dealt in the name of our nations, O God,
death in war, death through need and starvation
and death through tyrants of oppression.

Silent reflection

For everything of death which is done in our name, forgive us,
    Jesus Christ.
Forgive us and restore our life this day.
For we bow in grief before your goodness.

We are sad for other children
who have a hard life
because people don't love them enough.

Silent reflection and drumming

We are sorry, Jesus Christ.
Forgive us and restore our life this day.

Words of assurance

Even as he approaches his death,
Jesus cries out into the world that we are forgiven.
Let us pause in silence to honour this amazing gift which is ours:

A silence is kept

On this day, of all days, we are forgiven.
Thanks be to God.

O God, the Christ who has given everything for us and for all
people,
what more can we ask of you today?

Silent reflection

In humble faith we simply ask that you will gather us again
into your Body, made frail by its tough journey among us.
Gather all that is vulnerable in us,
and all that struggles in the pain of human existence.
Hold all our deaths within your death, O Christ.

Hold in your open arms
all who feel unloved by life and by those around them
that they may be held close to you
and know that someone cries with them.
Hold all our deaths within your death, O Christ,
as we wait in fragile hope for the day of risen life.
Amen.

Commissioning

Go silently from here,
for there are no words which will speak of this moment in the life
of God.

Benediction

Go blessed by the company of God, who dies rather than leave
us alone.
Go blessed by the faithfulness of Christ, who chooses life in the
face of death,
and go as those who stay with the truth, even as we wait for
Easter Day.
Amen.

EASTER DAY

We believe in the power of Christ
to overcome all deaths,
deaths in us and death in the world.

We believe in life which rises in freedom
and carries us in joy towards grace
beyond our imagining,
calling our spirits to soar in freedom
with wings of hope,
borne high in the wonder of Easter Day.

The gift of life will never be taken from us.
The costly life of God will be our company
for ever and for ever.

Rise up and live

—⟫•⟪—

Call to worship

Rise up and live!
Life springing forth from death is offered to the world.
Thanks be to you, O Christ.

Christ is risen, alive in overflowing grace.
Thanks be to you, O Christ.

Christ is risen, alive in the determined survival of good.
Thanks be to you, O Christ.
Death is overcome for ever.

Prayer of invocation

As we wait in awe this day,
we pray that the signs of the risen Christ
will be made real among us.
Be present with us in ways which go deeply into our life, O God,
that we may find the passion of your life within us and around us.
This we pray in faith
because we believe that you are indeed alive.
Amen.

Prayer of confession

Living God, even as we announce your rising,
we confess that hidden within our lives
lie questions which challenge our faith and your victory.
Doubts beset us as we look at the world around us,
fears that we may be wrong in holding to faith
when your life among us seems so often to be defeated.
Forgive our doubts, O God.
Spring forth in truth before us, we pray.

Then there are the times, O God,
when we choose to stay with our own deaths,
rather than accepting your gift of life to us.
We hold onto our old guilts.
We stay paralysed before our fears.
We are stricken by events long past
which you call us to leave behind us.
Forgive our doubts, O God.
Spring forth in truth before us, we pray,
that we may share more fully your risen life.
Amen.

Words of assurance

On this day, the day of the risen life of God,
we affirm that God loves us and will never bow to our deaths,
not even the deaths of guilt and shame.
We are forgiven.
The offer rings through the clouds of life
and into the sunshine of this moment.
Receive the life of Christ!
Thanks be to God.

Prayer of thanksgiving

What words will ever be enough, O God?
What songs can we sing to shout aloud our praise?
The universe springs up in joy at the sound of your voice,
assuring the world that the winter of death
gives way to the summer warmth of life.
We thank you that we cannot destroy you,
the Divine in all that lives.
We thank you that you give us this living sign
that the Christ will be among us for ever.
Amen.

Readings

Jeremiah 31.1–6; Psalm 118.1–2, 14–24; Colossians 3.1–4;
John 20.1–18

Sermon

Affirmation of faith

In response to the word, let us stand and affirm our faith together:

We believe in the power of Christ
to overcome all deaths,
deaths in us and death in the world.

We believe in life which rises in freedom
and carries us in joy towards grace
beyond our imagining,
calling our spirits to soar in freedom
with wings of hope
borne high in the wonder of Easter Day.

The gift of life will never be taken from us.
The costly life of God will be our company
for ever and for ever.

Prayer of intercession

On this day when we celebrate your risen life, O Christ,
we think of all the places and people
who rarely share in that joy
because their own lives are bowed down
with the weight of war, of want
and the domination of oppressive powers.
We remember them before you now:

The people pray and light candles

Lift up your risen life among them, we pray.
Rise in righteous indignation,
rise in courage and strength,
rise in justice which knows no end.

And then emerge as risen life in our lives, O Christ,
for we are always part of the future of others who suffer.

Silent reflection

Show your life in our life, O God.
Rise as clear commitment to those who struggle.

Rise as daring in facing the truth about ourselves
and the society in which we live.
Rise as brave stands for peace and compassion
and as faithfulness in never giving up on ourselves and others.

Rise in an end to apathy and hopelessness
and in celebration of your vision for a world we have not yet seen.
Be alive in us this day and every day, Jesus Christ,
for we long to be the people of the living God.
Amen.

Commissioning

Let us go with a song in our hearts,
bringing to all we meet the melody of love
which has been given to us in the rising of the Christ.

Benediction

And may the power of life in Christ lift up the life of the world,
the power of love in the Creator swing wide above us like the blue
    of the sky
and the faithfulness of the Holy Spirit raise our faith to the heights
    of hope.
Amen.

The fabric of life

This service is designed to follow the Good Friday service 'The torn fabric' and is set with the shroud and cross and torn fabric still in the sanctuary or centre of the church.

For this service you will need

- *A white sheet for a shroud*
- *A large cross*
- *Pieces of torn fabric*

Call to worship

We have seen, we have known,
the Christ is risen!
We have seen the rising of our God
in the fabric of our lives
rewoven in costly grace.

The pieces of fabric are taken from the cross and gathered into a basket

We have known the risen Christ
in love which does not falter,
in joy which cannot be defeated,
in passion that never dies.
Christ is risen,
Christ is risen indeed!

The cross is lifted from the floor and placed in an elevated position

Prayer of invocation

Even as we announce your rising, we are searching, O God,
often searching among the tombs of our life

for the signs of your life, wondering if you are really alive.
Come to meet us, with greetings on your lips,
come and leap free from the torn and broken
and be known to us as we gather in faith.
Amen.

The shroud is placed on the table as a cloth

Prayer of confession

Stay with us, loving Jesus.
Stay with us as you did on Good Friday
and do not leave us as we turn outward and look upon the world,
with its seemingly lost battles for good,
and the harsh mysteries of its injustices to the innocent.
Stay with us in that tough place, Jesus Christ,
with the warm heartbeat of your risen life.

A silence is kept

And then, as our doubting minds still falter,
in the face of all within us that would deny Godly life,
go before us towards every place which lies ahead, O Christ,
and forgive us for our lack of faith,
for we stand in longing hope before you.
Amen.

Words of assurance

This is the time when we live as though our sins are truly forgiven,
because Christ is alive and death is defeated for ever.
Receive the grace of God
and carry the news of the grace you have received
to all who will hear.
This is Good News for all the people!
Thanks be to God.

Readings

Jeremiah 31.1–6; Psalm 118.1–2, 14–24; Acts 10.34–43; Matthew 28.1–10

Sermon

Prayer of intercession

Go ahead of us, O God, into the Galilees of our day,
into the places where we try to make a difference,
or the places where life has become commonplace
and where new possibilities are forgotten.
Hear our prayer:
Colour the fabric of our life with your beauty.

Silent prayer

Go ahead of us, gracious Jesus,
into the places where we fear to tread
because we can see few signs of change,
or violences and oppressions which seem beyond
your power, or our power, to change.
In faith, we pray for others:

The people pray

Hear our prayer:
Colour the fabric of our lives with the excitement of faith.

And now, O God, we spread out the bright fabric of your life,
as we name the places where we believe we can see witnesses to
    your rising,
for celebration and the prayer that they may survive and grow
as a testimony to your presence in all the earth:

*The people place the torn pieces of cloth on the table as they name
the places and people who give them hope*

Let us celebrate this day!
Christ has died.
Christ is risen!
Christ will come again.
Thanks be to God for ever!
Amen.

Commissioning

Go as those who are called to be Christ's witnesses to the ends of
the earth.
Go carrying life which springs forth in abundance in the meanest
places,
places which would deny the risen life of God.

Benediction

And may the Christ, who lives in the vivid colour of abundant
life, be with us,
the God, who so loves the world that we are never left alone,
be before us
and the Spirit, who takes our hands for all that life will bring,
be present to us.
Amen.

Come alive!

Call to worship

Hail to Jesus!
God whose life leaps free of deathly forces,
with wounded hands and side,
revealing the costliness
and ringing true in victory
as it stands deep within our human struggling journeys:
We worship you this day.

Hail to Jesus!
The Human One, the Godly One,
joined for ever in eternal mystery,

yet claiming hope which rises
from the very ground of earth's tombs:
We worship you, for this is Easter Day.

Prayer of invocation

Risen Christ, show to us now, we pray,
the wonder of your living presence,
not in wisps or doubtful glimpses,
but in the glory of life hard won,
sweeping through our souls in splendour
and beyond us into a waiting world.
This we pray in faith and hope.
Amen.

Prayer of confession

Dear God, if we are tempted to watch your rising
as though it is a bright picture
painted for our momentary enjoyment,
separated from our everyday life:
Forgive us now and enter every part of our life with grace.

When we find it hard to believe in the power of your rising
because so many things around us
go on as if nothing has happened:
Forgive us now and enter every part of our life with grace.

If we see the victory of your resurrection
as salvation for ourselves alone,
and fail to share in your dream
of bringing to every system of oppression,
and every force on earth which destroys,
the justice, peace and compassion which is the sign of your reign:
Forgive us now and enter every part of our life with grace.
Stay with us now, risen Christ, we pray.
Amen.

Words of assurance

Nothing can separate us from the love of God.
Even death itself bows before the power of costly grace.
We are forgiven!
Thanks be to God.

Prayer of thanksgiving

Our spirits sing in joy, O God.
Thankfulness spreads through all the earth
like bursts of golden sunshine springing forth
among the grey-green colours of our trembling hopes.
Liberation from cynicism and apathy blossoms red in gladness,
celebrating a different future, a vision splendid,
in the face of your determination to bring new life to the world.
Thanks be to you, O God, for the miracle of Easter.
Amen.

Readings

Isaiah 65.17–25; Psalm 118.1–2, 14–24; 1 Corinthians 15.19–26;
John 20.1–18

Sermon

Prayer of intercession

Make real your risen life among us, O Christ.
Stretch it out across the heavens like stars of light
which show us where your truth might lie
in the dark places of suffering.

The people pray for these places

Warm our struggling world, O Christ,
where hearts lie cold in calculated self-interest,
showering your sparks of compassion
and the flames of justice
into the ashes of unlikely places.

The people pray about issues that concern them

Show to those who are ill, or wounded by life,
your outstretched wounded hands,
that they may believe that you know and care
and accompany them in every day of their lives.

The people pray for particular people

Pour love down like fruitful rain, O Christ,
over the dry places of our life,
so that the hidden seeds of our small ideas
may open into new greening
and bring forth the flowers of transforming hope.

The people pray about their hopes

Embrace your church, O God,
so that we may know your life-giving love so profoundly
that our celebration flows over and covers the groaning creation
with the wonder of your abundance.
Christ has died.
Christ is risen.
Christ will come again.
Amen.

Commissioning

Go into all the world as those
who are filled with the risen life of Jesus Christ
and the bearers of grace.

Benediction

And may the wonder of Easter break forth anew in us,
in those we love and in all the earth,
on this day and in the days to come.
In the name of the Great Creator, the risen Christ and the
    Holy Spirit of God,
Amen.

PENTECOST

The fire of the life of God burns around us,
in passion for change,
in energy for a new creation.
The flames of the Spirit rise into the air
springing from a warming hope,
leaping in life that will not be stilled.
The coals of glowing life
remain when we think they have long gone,
waiting for the kindling of commitment,
in the imagination of God.

The power of the Spirit

For this service you will need

- *A red candle*
- *A long flowing red cloth*
- *A number of small candles for lighting*

Call to worship

Holy, holy, holy God,
wonder, mystery and all-goodness,
in the power of the Spirit we are carried into your presence:
You are our God and we are your people.

A red candle is lit on the table

Holy, holy, holy God,
healer, liberator and all-justice,
in the power of the Spirit we are called into the world:
You are our God and we are your people,
and we come to worship you in faith and in hope.

The long red cloth is placed from the candle, flowing towards the door

Prayer of invocation

Be alive among us this day, Jesus Christ,
drawing all eyes towards your word as it is revealed before us,
opening all ears as your Spirit speaks into our hearts
and moving within our lives in ways which touch us deeply
so that we bow in humble faith before your holiness.
Come to us now, we pray, O God.
Amen.

Prayer of confession

Dear God, if our faith has become so mundane to us
that we have ceased to expect to be surprised by your holiness,
treading each day as if we know all that is possible
instead of looking around us for your new word:
Stride into our lives, Jesus Christ,
and interrupt us with your grace.

O God, when we look at others and fail to see the godliness
which may be present there,
assuming that we know all there is to know about them
and closing our minds and hearts to fresh gifts:
Stride into our lives, Jesus Christ,
and interrupt us with your grace.

O God, if we rarely search ourselves
to see if you are inviting the sharing of beauty and wisdom
from within our own lives
and inspiring us to be the vehicles for your holy word in this day:
Stride into our lives, Jesus Christ,
and interrupt us with your grace.
Forgive us when we expect less than you give.
Amen.

Assurance of pardon

Turn your lives towards the Holy God,
for all grace is there, all freedom and hope.
The word of God will not fail us.
We are forgiven.
Thanks be to God.
Amen.

Prayer of thanksgiving

We thank you, O God,
for moments undeserved and unexpected,
blessings which we have not planned to receive,
and gifts from those we have not noticed before.

We thank you, O God,
that you are always grander and greater than we will ever know,
that we can never truly name who you are,
never do justice to the breadth of your love.
We bring you thanks, O God, this day and every day.
Amen.

Readings

Nehemiah 8.1–3, 5–6, 8–10; Psalm 19; 1 Corinthians 12.12–31a;
Luke 4.14–21

Sermon

Prayer of intercession

Jesus Christ, true Messiah for all time,
you have announced a new creation for all people
where the captives leap free,
the suffering are healed
and the poor hear good news.
We pray, O God, that we will believe that this is possible,
that we will look at the world with new eyes
as though many things could change,
as though the powers which seem invincible
will bow to your will.

Silent reflection

Help us in our unbelief, O God.
Help us when our faith turns to apathy or cynicism.
Help us when we hardly know what to pray
in case you ask of us more than we can give.

Silent reflection

As a sign of our faith this day, Jesus Christ,
we bring before you these our prayers for others and ourselves:

The people pray

Let us place small candles along the cloth
as we name places and situations where we believe
that things could change for good in the power of God.

The people do so

Raise up different ways for our journeying, O God,
ways of living so closely with the power of your Spirit
that we see and act in response to your truth,
even though we cannot perceive your good future.
**This we pray as your humble human people, O God.
Amen.**

Commissioning

Go forth and point to the wonders of God.
Go forth and carry justice and compassion into the world,
for this is the word in Christ to us.

Benediction

And may God rise up in majesty before us,
Christ Jesus draw our eyes towards true life
and the Holy Spirit be discovered in every new day.
Amen.

I come to bring fire

Call to worship

The fire of the life of God burns around us,
in passion for change,
in energy for a new creation.
The flames of the Spirit rise into the air

springing from a warming hope,
leaping in life that will not be stilled.
The coals of glowing life
remaining when we think they have long gone,
waiting for the kindling of commitment,
in the imagination of God.
Let us worship our God.

Prayer of invocation

Breathe your vivid life into our life, O God.
Colour our horizons with the rays of your new ideas
as we meet this day.
Make yourself known to us in warmed hearts
and risen hopes.
For we wait on you in humble faith.
Amen.

Prayer of confession

O God, we love to dwell on your kindness to us,
on the gentle shepherd, Christ.
When you come to us in indignation,
in fiery determination and confront our complacency,
we confess that we are tempted to turn away
or pretend that we have not noticed.

Silent reflection

Forgive us, O God.
Stand before us in light and fire to warm our lives.

If we tend to look at those who disturb our peace
as troublemakers, as do-gooders
or as people who are being too political,
hold our minds open to look at them with wisdom
in case they are the bearers of your word.
If we refuse to engage with the stirring of uneasiness,
the challenge to what we know:

Forgive us, O God.
Stand before us in light and fire to warm our lives.

When our lives are reduced down into small issues,
when we become preoccupied with things that are insignificant,
losing your perspective in our feverish little causes:
Forgive us, O God.
Stand before us in light and fire to warm our lives.
Confront us with the truth through your Holy Spirit.
Amen.

Words of assurance

Even the Christ is challenged by the task before us.
Take heart and believe that God knows our every struggle
and still brings us grace.
We are forgiven.
Thanks be to God.

Prayer of thanksgiving

We lift up our hearts before you, O God.
Our souls breathe free in the wonder of your life,
expanding outwards into new possibilities.
We give you thanks for being a God
who is never satisfied with dull acceptance of what is
and yet, in the wonder of your life,
still offers us peace when we need it for our survival.
We give you thanks this day, O God.
Amen.

Readings

Isaiah 5.1–7; Psalm 80.1–2, 8–19; Hebrews 11.29—12.2; Luke
12.49–56

Sermon

Offering

Prayer of intercession

O God, it is daunting to believe
that your work in the world depends on us.
Gather around us today all that we need to be your people,
    we pray.
May we not be overwhelmed by the examples before us,
but be encouraged by the faith that they too
were just ordinary human beings like us.
May our lives be inspired and expanded by their lives,
made grander in the visions which lie before us,
made even more dependent on your courage and strength
as we face the world in our day.

A silence is kept

As we dare to look at the struggles of our time,
this is what we see, O God.
These are the places and people for whom we pray.
These are the situations which call to us in longing:

The people pray

Be with us, O God.
Make music in us, Holy Spirit,
that the melodies of your life may drown out
the murmurings of our doubt and fear.
Paint your pictures of creativity around our life, O God,
source of all the universe
and then take us by the hand, Jesus Christ,
and lead us past our trembling into the glory of your dream
    for us.
We pray this in your name.
Amen.

Commissioning

Carry the flame of Christ's life into all the world.
Go in peace and go in the confidence of faith.

Benediction

And may the forces of oppression bow before the courage
    of Christ,
the corruptions of power be challenged by the grace of God
and the Holy Spirit be found in all the earth.
Amen.

Send forth the Spirit

Call to worship

The Holy Spirit of Christ takes wing
and flies in delight among all that lives.
She soars in love in the centre of struggling earth,
inviting us, calling to us,
enchanting us with fresh visions of good.
He hovers over our heads this Pentecost Day
as God's dove of peace
and touches our hearts with hopes for a kinder world.
Let us worship our God
and celebrate with joy the coming of the Holy Spirit.

Prayer of invocation

Breathe the mystery of your life into our midst, Spirit of God,
enlarging our dreams,
enhancing our love for each other and the world.
Speak to us in ways which cut through our fears and doubts
to sound as music in our souls
and light in us a fiery passion to be your brave people.
Come, Holy Spirit, come.

Prayer of confession

O God of colourful life,
we often appear to be rather pale in our living,
washed out by our hesitations in following in your prophetic way,
and drab in our tentative commitments to your justice
or even colourless as we stand paralysed by doubt.
Come, Holy Spirit, come.
Visit us with your grace upon grace and bring us back to life.

We also own that sometimes we try to hold your lithe Spirit,
trying to capture you in our neat rules,
or believing that we can keep you in company of our own
   choosing.
Come, Holy Spirit, come.
Visit us with your grace upon grace and bring us back to life.

If we defend ourselves against the challenge of your vivid life,
   Holy Spirit,
raising barriers to your call
so that we can stay in comfortable places:
Come, Holy Spirit, come.
Visit us with your grace upon grace
and bring us back to life, we pray.
Amen.

Words of assurance

Wait in wonder for the gifts of the Spirit,
gifts of healing and comfort,
gifts of forgiveness and love.
Wait in wonder and faith
for the Holy Spirit has indeed come to all who believe.
We are forgiven.
Thanks be to God.

Prayer of thanksgiving

This is the day of our salvation,
this and every day.
This is the moment when God surprises us
with gifts beyond our asking.
Our hearts will sing with gratitude.
Our minds will grasp God's new way
and our souls will be lifted up in joy.
This is the Day of Pentecost!
Thanks be to God.
Amen.

Readings

Acts 2.1–21; Psalm 104.24–34, 35b; Romans 8.14–17; John 14.8–17

Sermon

Prayer of intercession

This is the day when we celebrate the gifts of the Holy Spirit
which descend upon the people.
Let us give thanks to God for the gifts which we already perceive
    among us:

The people name the gifts

May we graciously affirm the gifts in each other, O God,
encouraging those which are barely glimpsed,
applauding those which are hard won
and tenderly cherishing those which are fragile.

And now let us ask our God for the gifts which are needed
for our ministry in this place,
those which would enrich our ministry in the world
and within our own life:

The people pray for particular gifts

We will never be enough for all that is to be done, O God,
but we wait in hope to receive all that you offer to us.
Give to us the wisdom which we need
to use your gifts with courage and humility.
Speak to us in words which we can understand,
making clear the way before us with signposts of your love.
We believe that nothing is impossible with you, Holy Spirit,
nothing is lost or wasted
and nothing goes unnoticed in your eternal love for us
and for the world.
Be with us as we go, we pray.
Amen.

Commissioning

Go in gladness as those who have been given
far more than we will ever earn or deserve.

Benediction

And may the flame of the Holy Spirit warm the cold places,
the wind of the Holy Spirit sweep away all that holds us back
and the dove of peace hover over the world in reconciling
gentleness.
Amen.

EUCHARISTS

We gather around this table, the table of Christ.
We claim our place here
as ordinary human beings,
all equal in the eyes of God,
none more worthy than the other
to share in the feast.

The gift of the unexpected – the Eucharist

Offertory

No one comes as a stranger to this holy table.
All of us are honoured and expected guests.
Each of us is invited to come as we are,
holding nothing in our hands
other than these humble offerings of bread and wine,
the food and drink of ordinary life made with human hands
from the gifts which lie in God's creation.
Receive our gifts, we pray, O God.
Amen.

The great thanksgiving

Christ be with you.
And also with you.

Lift up your hearts!
We lift them up to God.

Let us give thanks to God.
It is right to give our thanks and praise.

We thank you, O God,
for the pausing and the waiting,
the going down deep into our lives
which reveals to us unexpected love
from you, from others and even from ourselves.

We thank you that there never is a time
when we know all that there is to know,
when we have received all that is to come
or have seen all that there is to see.

We thank you that, in the face of certainty,
you bring in a whole new day
and that as the barriers to good seem to enclose us,
you break life open in miracles of grace.

We give you thanks that the vulnerable Child, Jesus,
is placed in human hands and takes human life,
that we may believe that a grander love
may arise from within our midst.

And so we praise you
with the faithful of every time and place,
joining with the whole creation in the eternal hymn:

**Holy, holy, holy, God of power and vulnerability,
heaven and earth are full of your glory.
Come and deliver us, God the giver of life.
Blessed is the One who comes in the name of our God.
Come and deliver us, God the giver of life.**

The institution

The invocation

The Lord's prayer

The breaking of the bread

This is the bread of life
and this is the wine of compassion.
The gifts of God for the people of God.

Final prayer

O God, we give you grateful thanks
for all that lies within this sacred feast.
**May our lives show the signs
that love is possible,**

grace is believable
and compassion is our way of life.
This we pray in your name.
Amen.

Sending out and blessing

Go as those who have received the abundant feast of God.
And may the hand of the Christ
rest upon our heads in blessing,
the touch of the Holy Spirit
reach out towards us in encouragement
and God the Loving Parent hold us and protect us.
Amen.

Bread of life and wine of compassion

Offertory

The holy table of Jesus Christ waits for its honoured guests:
all of us, each of us who come in humble faith.
It waits with openness to receive our gifts,
the gifts which arise from the crushing of the seeds
and the trampling of the grapes,
formed through the work of human hands
into the bread and wine which we will offer to God
for transformation into even grander gifts for us.

Receive these our offerings now, O God,
and greet us in grace as we approach your holy table.
Amen.

The great thanksgiving

Christ be with you.
And also with you.

Lift up your hearts!
We lift them up to God.

Let us give thanks to God.
It is right to give our thanks and praise.

We give you thanks, O God, for Jesus Christ,
who held the people tenderly in his hands
and healed and comforted them.

We thank you for his loving acceptance
of the little and the least,
the struggling and the rejected,
and people like ourselves
who hold within our lives
hard questions for life and faith.

We give you thanks for echoes in our journeys
which make true the gospel of Jesus Christ
and the testimony of his life,
a life which travelled in courage towards deathliness
and showed us the pathway into passionate life.

We give you thanks for our life together,
the Body of Christ in this place
which claims in faith, against many a doubt,
that risen life lies in our midst
and will stay with us for ever.

And so we praise you
with the faithful of every time and place,
joining with the whole creation
in the eternal hymn:

**Holy, holy, holy, God of power and vulnerability,
heaven and earth are full of your glory.**

Come and deliver us, God the giver of life.
Blessed is the One who comes in the name of our God.
Come and deliver us, God the giver of life.

The institution

The invocation

The Lord's prayer

The breaking of the bread

This is the bread of life
and this is the wine of compassion.
The gifts of God for the people of God.

Final prayer

O God, we give you grateful thanks
for all that lies within this sacred feast.
May we carry into the world
the bread which brings life
and the wine of compassion
for all who wait in longing.
This we pray in your name.
Amen.

Blessing

Go as those who have received the abundant feast of God.
And may the hand of the Christ
rest upon our heads in blessing,
the touch of the Holy Spirit
reach out towards us in encouragement
and God the Loving Parent hold us and protect us.
Amen.

Glimpses of God

Offering

The holy table of Jesus Christ waits for its honoured guests:
all of us, each of us who come in humble faith.
Here lies the hospitality of God,
the open heart of Christ
and the dancing life of the Holy Spirit.
Into this feast we bring our offerings.
Receive them now, O God,
and greet us in grace as we approach your holy table.
Amen.

The great thanksgiving

Christ be with you.
And also with you.

Lift up your hearts!
We lift them up to God.

Let us give thanks to God.
It is right to give our thanks and praise.

Thanks be to you, O God,
for the wonder of the threads of hope
which you weave through all creation.
Thanks be to you for small signs
which you give to us each day, if only we will look:
for fragile flowers in forest and meadow,
for colour in a rock
and a smile on the face of a child.
Thanks be to you, O God.

Thanks be to you for gifts which wait for us
if we will see them:

in a small kindness from one to another,
in a standing back to allow us to go through first,
or a word of insight from an unexpected place.
Thank you for a brave laugh surviving in sadness
and for faithful love which stands the test of every day.
Thanks be to you for your gifts to us, O God.

We give you thanks that as we stay
and go down deep into the heart of Christ
we may go past our own shadow places
and gently stand on the ground of truth.
We thank you that there, in surprising grace, lies peace,
waiting within our own longings.

And so we praise you
with the faithful of every time and place,
joining with the whole creation
in the eternal hymn:

**Holy, holy, holy, God of power and vulnerability,
heaven and earth are full of your glory.
Come and deliver us, God the giver of life.
Blessed is the One who comes in the name of our God.
Come and deliver us, God the giver of life.**

The institution

The invocation

The Lord's prayer

The breaking of the bread

This is the life of God,
broken and poured out for us.
The gifts of God for the people of God.

Final prayer

O God, we give you grateful thanks
for all that lies within this sacred feast.
May our lives show the signs
that love is possible,
grace is believable
and compassion is our way of life.
This we pray in your name.
Amen.

Sending out and blessing

Go as those who have received the abundant feast of God.
And may the hand of the Christ
rest upon our heads in blessing,
the touch of the Holy Spirit
reach out towards us in encouragement
and God the Loving Parent hold us and protect us.
Amen.

Journey into compassion

This liturgy was prepared for use after a time of meditation,
self-awareness or retreat.

Opening

To close the spaces between ourselves and God
begins with compassion for our vulnerable selves
as a sign that we have faith that God is indeed gracious.
In this spirit of compassion we will today
dare to remember our own truths,

honour our grieving, angers, pain and fears,
claim our own dignity,
cherish ourselves and celebrate our existence,
believing that we are embraced by a goodness and love
which is within and beyond ourselves – in each other and in God.

Silent reflection

Offertory

Here we will bring the ordinary things of life,
the bread and the wine
and any gifts which lie in the midst of humanness.
Receive them, loving God,
and add to them your holiness and your wholeness.
Amen.

The great thanksgiving

Christ be with you.
And also with you.

Lift up your hearts!
We lift them up to God.

Let us give thanks to God.
It is right to give our thanks and praise.

We praise and thank you, Holy God,
for the rain that falls on the just and unjust,
for your respecting of the struggles of your creation,
even our struggles,
and for the ripples of your grace
which flow forth eternally in all that is.

We thank you for Jesus Christ,
who walked within all of our reality,
stood in the centre of our betrayals
and with all integrity
claimed the glory of life,
hard won, and coloured deep
with the blood of our pain.

God in the torn apart,
God in the wholeness,
God in the emptiness,
God in the fullness,
you are God with us
in everlasting faithfulness.

And so we praise you
with the faithful of every time and place,
joining with the whole creation in the eternal hymn:

Holy, holy, holy Lord,
God of power and vulnerability,
heaven and earth are full of your glory.
Hosanna in the highest.
Blessed is the One who comes in the name of our God.
Hosanna in the highest.

The institution

The invocation

The breaking of the bread

The bread we break is a sharing in the body of Christ.
The cup we take is a sharing in the life-blood of Christ.
For as Christ shares our brokenness,
so we share in God's wholeness.
As life is poured out in costly love,
so eternal grace is there for us and for all people.
The gifts of God for the people of God.

The distribution

The affirmation

We are a good creation, a beautiful people.
We will not be destroyed or defeated

because the divine love is stronger than any deaths.
In thanksgiving,
we will celebrate our compassion for ourselves
and our freedom to love others,
in ways which are true to us.
We will claim in full the loving energies
which lie in the universe itself, and in God,
and move into a new day.
Amen.

The blessing

Go in peace, for that is rightfully ours.
Go in love, the love which is our birthright.
Go in courage, for Jesus Christ walks with us.
Amen.

The feast for all

Offertory

The bread, wine and offerings are placed on the table

We place on this table our offerings:
our gifts, which will be used
in the grander hospitality of God.
Our gifts will be received by God
and joined with those around the world
as they spread outwards towards those
who long and wait for love and justice.

We gather around this table, the table of Christ.
We claim our place here

as ordinary human beings,
all equal in the eyes of God,
none more worthy than the other
to share in the feast.

The great thanksgiving

Christ be with you.
And also with you.

Lift up your hearts!
We lift them up to God.

Let us give thanks to God.
It is right to give our thanks and praise.

We thank you, loving God,
that Jesus calls the people of faith
in every age and place,
to break down the barriers which separate people,
to relate to each other with humility and respect,
to share kindness with every person,
to struggle to bring justice to life in every place
and to welcome all people to the feast of life.

We thank you that we can approach this table,
no matter who we are or who we have been,
no matter what our confusions or how deep our doubts.
We thank you, O God, that Jesus Christ
lived in ways which revealed you to be
a God who calls us on
to life which is greater and grander
than we have ever known.

And so we praise you
with the faithful of every time and place,
joining with the whole creation
in the eternal hymn:

Holy, holy, holy, God of power and vulnerability,
heaven and earth are full of your glory.
Come and deliver us, God the giver of life.
Blessed is the One who comes in the name of our God.
Come and deliver us, God the giver of life.

The institution

The invocation

The Lord's prayer

The breaking of the bread

The distribution

Come, take your place at the table of God,
the open table of grace and love.
Come, stand in a circle
where no one is more significant than another.

The people do so

Final prayer

We thank you that we are the guests at your table, O God.
We pray that one day no one will be left out,
that all will gather and share the feast of God.
We pray that our gratitude for what we have received
will make us part of the changing of the world.
Amen.

Dismissal and blessing

Go as those who are the faithful witnesses to God's kindness.
And may those who have little be blessed with abundance,
those who have much be blessed with generosity
and all creation give thanks to its Maker.
Amen.

FOR
SPECIAL OCCASIONS

Yes, we have a grave task in ministry.
Yes, we are tested and tried in many ways.
Yes, we will never know what each day may bring
or what the future holds.
All this lies within the circle of God's love.

We are also those who laugh and play,
those who discover wonderful gifts among us,
those who eat and drink in celebration,
who sing and make music together,
whose hearts are lifted by our life,
among the wonder of the creation
and the delights of living.
We will celebrate this day.
Thanks be to God!

Celebrating our life –
a service to open a meeting of chaplains

For this worship you will need

- *A cloth spread on the floor or on a table with stones clustered and dotted across it*
- *A basket of flowers*

Opening sentences

Yes, we have a grave task in ministry.
Yes, we are tested and tried in many ways.
Yes, we will never know what each day may bring
or what the future holds.
All this lies within the circle of God's love.

We are also those who laugh and play,
those who discover wonderful gifts among us,
those who eat and drink in celebration,
who sing and make music together,
whose hearts are lifted by our life,
among the wonder of the creation
and the delights of living.
We will celebrate this day.
Thanks be to God!

Flowers among the stones

Among the stones lie the moments of joy,
the colour of growing, of surprising gifts
and of the simple beauty in our life together.
Let us take a flower, name it and place it among the stones:

The people do so

Our neediness, our failures and the struggle of the people
among whom we minister,
is never the whole truth about our life and work.
**With thankful hearts, O God,
we celebrate a greater truth
in the signs of your abundant life among us.
Open our eyes and hearts, we pray,
that we may always see your spreading grace
which flows in healing and nurturing life
among the stones.**

Reading

Isaiah 55.10–13

Prayers for our life

Let us each share one thing in our life and work for which we
would like special prayers:

The people do so

After each request for prayer:

We have heard the prayer which you bring.
**We join you in that prayer
and place it before God in faith.**

Hold our lives in your hand, gracious God.
**We dedicate our ministries to you afresh
and commit ourselves to each other and to you,
in the name of Christ.
Amen.**

Sending out into life and work

Go from here in faith,
sure in the love of God and each other.

And may the Holy God surprise us on the way,
Christ Jesus be our company
and the Holy Spirit break open life before us.
Amen.

Opening a meeting –
surprised by God

———◆———

Opening sentences

In every beginning, in every moment,
God may surprise us with new possibilities,
new courage and wisdom
and new dimensions of faith.
This is our God,
Creator, Christ and Holy Spirit.
Let us be the people of God this day.

We are human

O God, we are your very human people
and we confess that we do not always expect
to be challenged by your creativity,
or your prophetic word.
We often think and act as though we know the future,
we know what is expected of us
and do what we always do.

Silent reflection

Forgive us if we have lost the dream of your life.
Bring to us your surprising grace, Jesus Christ.
Amen.

Assurance

The rock of God's faithfulness never fails us,
the forgiveness of Jesus Christ comes in grace upon grace
and the Holy Spirit will lift up our life.
Let us choose to live abundantly!
Amen.

Reading

Suggested reading: the Gospel for the week

Affirmation

In response to the word, let us make our affirmation:
We believe that God is present here,
meeting us within our meeting,
speaking into every heart,
offering wisdom for every mind
and breathing hope into every soul.
We believe that, in Christ,
all things are possible
and in the Spirit
all life is being made new.
This we believe.

Intercession

Loving God, take all that we do
and give to it the grandeur of your will,
the wonder of Christ's abundant life
and the truth and power of your Holy Spirit.
Carry our life into the world which you so love,
that we may be part of the bringing in of your reign,
witnesses to your justice and peace
and friends to all who long for love.
This we pray in your name.
Amen.

Blessing

May the Holy God guide us in the pathways of truth,
Christ Jesus gather us into loving community as his Body
and the Spirit inspire us and call us on into joy.
Amen.

Social Justice Sunday – for such a time as this

⇒•◦•⇐

This service is focused on accepting diversity.

For this service you will need

- *Symbols of some of the different races and cultures which are present either in the congregation or in the community. These could be cultural objects, cloth, art or craft, pictures of different people or simply names on cards*
- *A candle*

Call to worship

At such a time as this,
you are our God.
All time is your time,
and all history is gathered into your life.
All people are your good creation,
embraced in your love for the world
and we celebrate the wonder of that.
On this day, we come to worship you.
**We will worship you
in spirit and in truth, O God.**

The celebration

Let us image the beauty of God's good creation.
We will place on the holy table
signs of the diversity of humankind.

The symbols are placed

The circle of God's community is never complete
until we are all an honoured part.

We now light this candle, the sign of the light of Christ
which shines forth among all people.

The candle is lit

Invocation

Reveal your life among us, O God,
speak to us in ways beyond our imagining, Christ Jesus
and be present to us in friend and stranger.
Come, Holy Spirit, come.
Amen.

Confession

At such a time as this, O God,
we stand before your holiness in grief
and own that we have not always
loved our neighbour as ourselves.
We have failed to create a world
in which all people are loved and accepted.
We have found it hard to see beyond differences
into the common humanity which we share.

Silent reflection

Forgive us, loving God.
Forgive us and bring us to a grander hope.

Sometimes, O God, we have decided that we are superior
to people of races and cultures other than our own,
presuming to judge your handiwork
which is expressed in our diversity.

Silent reflection

Forgive us, loving God.
Forgive us and bring us to a grander hope.

At other times, O God, we have put boundaries on your call to us,
shutting out disturbing news of suffering,
telling ourselves that it is not our concern,
as though the community which you invite us to enter
is narrow and confined to those we find most comfortable.

Silent reflection

Forgive us, loving God.
**Forgive us and bring us to a grander hope
that we may more truly be your people.
Amen.**

Assurance of pardon

The Holy God never fails to offer grace in Jesus Christ,
never loses faith in new possibilities for our next day.
We are indeed forgiven, each of us and all of us.
Thanks be to God.

Readings

Isaiah 42.5–9; Ephesians 1.15–19; Matthew 25.31–45
These could be read in several languages

Sermon

Affirmation of faith

In response to the word, let us affirm our faith:
**We believe in God
who created all that is in infinite variety,
full of colour, grace and gifts.**

**We believe in Jesus Christ,
ever moving towards the edges of life,
gathering in the little and the least,
inviting them to the table of joy,
and walking beside them on the way.**

**We believe in the Holy Spirit,
life of God within our life,
moving in each moment,
offering wisdom and newness
and dancing with new possibilities.**

Prayers of intercession

How will we pray in such a time as this?
How will we bring our world before our God
for healing, justice and compassion?

Silent reflection

O God, we pray for those who believe
that they are lesser human beings
because of the way they have been treated
by other races of people
and whose culture has been crushed
because it was different from that of those in power.

Specific prayers may be offered

Make us part of your new world, O God.
**Create in us brave hearts to make the changes in ourselves
and to invite the changes in others.**

O God, we pray for those who fear to walk the streets
because they may face abuse or violence,
and for children who do not feel welcome in school playgrounds.
We pray for young people who have become bitter and hurt
because they live between two cultures,
struggling to honour their history and their present.

Specific prayers may be offered

Make us part of your new world, O God.
**Create in us brave hearts to make the changes in ourselves
and to invite the changes in others.**

And now we pray for ourselves, O God.
Open our hearts to receive gifts from those who are different,
open our eyes to see you present within their lives,
open our ears to hear their stories
and open our mouths to be a voice for those who suffer in silence.
**May your church be a place of open arms and open minds,
embracing all those for whom you came, Jesus Christ.**

We pray this in your name.
Amen.

Sending out

Go in faith to be part of the new creation of human community.
Go in love to take the hand of those who long for inclusion.

Blessing

And may God the Creator speak to us in all creation,
Christ Jesus bring all people to the table
and the Holy Spirit be our constant companion at such a time
    as this.
Amen.

We are part of the tree of life –
a service for a retreat or parish camp
or workshop

*This service has also been used with long-term prisoners who feel
that they have no real existence or future. It invites them to claim
that they 'are', even if only a bit of shed bark alongside the tree.*

For this service you will need

- *A large piece of cotton cloth – perhaps a cheap bed sheet – with
an outline of a bare tree drawn on it, placed in the centre of
gathered people on the floor or on a table (be sure to place some
paper under it so that any writing doesn't go through on to the
surface beneath it)*
- *Fabric pens*
- *Basket of leaves – real or made of felt*

Opening sentences

Life flows forth from God,
like a tree beside the water,
sometimes standing gnarled by struggles
or wounded in hidden ways,
sometimes showing green shoots of survival
or a surprising flower of kindness.
The tree of life is hard won,
with birds of hope to be found within its branches.

We are part of life

We are a part of life.
We are the grieving and the moment of laughter.
We are the weeping and the sound of a song within.
We are the growing and the standing still,
the despairing and the fleeting promise of better,
the beginnings and the endings.
We are life, not the whole, but a true part.

We belong to the tree of life:
small pieces of its bark,
a tiny fragile twig,
a frail root unseen,
an old forgotten layer of its trunk,
a stone touching its base
or a bare hole in its side.
We are the seen and the unseen, all part of this tree.

Readings

Isaiah 43.1–4; Revelation 22.1–2

Reflection

Claiming our place

Let us image who we are
and then take our place as part of the tree of life,
or waiting alongside it ready to resume our place.
We may hold the image to ourselves
or share it by writing our name on the tree
and, if we wish, describing our place there.

The people do so

(*On another occasion people may be asked to look at each other and
choose a place for other people as part of the tree*)

Prayers for others

The leaves of the tree
are for the healing of the nations,
for the healing of the world by God
in company with us.

Let us hold a leaf in our hands and think about where healing
    is needed,
our healing and the healing of others.

A basket of leaves is passed around and a silence is kept

Let us pray for ourselves and others
and place our leaves on the tree of life,
or simply hold them to ourselves.

O God, send the water of life towards us all –
healing, forgiving and nourishing,
flowing over our lives in kindness and understanding,
spreading among us so that we grow and change
in ways which we could never imagine.
Support us, care for us, O God.
give to us the courage and strength
we need for this day
and the days which lie ahead.

We pray in humble faith.
Amen.

Sending out and blessing

Let us go into this day,
known and loved as we are.

And may we remember
that we are part of something larger,
sharers of life with Jesus Christ
and carried into a new future in the power of the Spirit.
Amen.

Placing the task in God's hands – a service of commitment for people facing a ministry among struggling people

For this service you will need

- *A long soft cloth or cloths with which to form a circle on the floor*
- *A basket of stones*

Opening sentences

The task of ministry is always larger than our gifts.
The task of this ministry is wider and deeper than most.
It is lived out with the most vulnerable,
it walks beside many who cannot even name their need,
it shares life with those who enter the abyss,
who are enclosed in a multitude of ways,

in grief, in pain, in prisons, in illness,
in loneliness and fear, in torments of the soul.
This is the glory and gravity of our ministry.
We will place it in the circle of God's love.

The circle is created with the cloth/s

We are never outside the hands of God.
God is with us and God will be with us.

Holding the people before our God

In this basket are stones,
the hardness of the life of the people we serve,
sometimes worn smooth by its harshness,
sometimes still rough to the touch.

I invite you to take one or two stones
and hold them in your hands.
In the silence, reflect on what it is you hold there.

A silence is kept

When you are ready,
name something of what lies in each stone
and place it within the circle of God's love.

The people do so

We are your ordinary human people, O God.
**Even as we have taken up this task,
we know we are never enough to do it.
We do not have enough love,
enough wisdom, enough strength and courage
or enough faithfulness.**

The circle of God's love gathers us in
among the people we serve.

Let us take another stone,
one which represents each one of us,

and place it beside the people
as a sign of our need of the love of God,
the company of the Christ
and the inspiration of the Holy Spirit.

The people do so

Reading

Isaiah 45.5–9

Prayer

O God, in faith we lay our own ministries
among those we serve.
Encircle us with your love and wisdom as we go.

Commitment

Before a loving God, let us commit ourselves to this task:
In hope and faith,
we offer our lives to God.
In joy and wonder,
we honour our calling
and, surrounded by prayer,
we will take up this ministry.
God is with us and God is within us.
Amen.

Sending into a new day

Go in faith and hope,
for we are never left alone.

And may God be known in each moment we share,
Christ Jesus create footsteps ahead for our walking
and the Spirit dance in delight in our joyful life together.
Amen.

The Society for Promoting Christian Knowledge (SPCK) was founded in 1698. Its mission statement is:

To promote Christian knowledge by
- **Communicating the Christian faith in its rich diversity;**
- **Helping people to understand the Christian faith and to develop their personal faith; and**
- **Equipping Christians for mission and ministry.**

SPCK Worldwide serves the Church through Christian literature and communication projects in over 100 countries, and provides books for those training for ministry in many parts of the developing world. This worldwide service depends upon the generosity of others and all gifts are spent wholly on ministry programmes, without deductions.

SPCK Bookshops support the life of the Christian community by making available a full range of Christian literature and other resources, providing support for those training for ministry, and assisting bookstalls and book agents throughout the UK.

SPCK Publishing produces Christian books and resources, covering a wide range of inspirational, pastoral, practical and academic subjects. Authors are drawn from many different Christian traditions, and publications aim to meet the needs of a wide variety of readers in the UK and throughout the world.

The Society does not necessarily endorse the individual views contained in its publications, but hopes they stimulate readers to think about and further develop their Christian faith.

For further information about the Society, visit our website at
www.spck.org.uk or write to:
SPCK, 36 Causton Street,
London SW1P 4ST, United Kingdom.